DIY COLOUR SERIES

HOME ELECTRICS

AURA
EDITIONS

CONTENTS

Editor: Helen Davies
Art editor: Graham Beehag

Published by Aura Editions
2 Derby Road, Greenford, Middlesex

Produced by Marshall Cavendish Books Limited
58 Old Compton Street, London W1V 5PA

© Marshall Cavendish Limited 1986

ISBN 0 86307 480 4

Phototypeset in 10/11 Garamond by Quadraset Limited, Midsomer Norton, Bath
Printed and bound in Italy by LEGO S.p.A.

While every care has been taken to ensure that the information in *Home Electrics* is accurate,
individual circumstances may vary greatly. So proceed with caution,
especially where electrical, plumbing or structural work is involved.

CHAPTER 1

BASIC SKILLS

Never approach any electrical job until you first have a solid
grasp of the basics—how your electrical system works, what
types of flex and cables to use and how to deal with blown fuses.
This is all essential information which will stand you in good
stead when you start your own electrical installations

ALL ABOUT HOME ELECTRICS

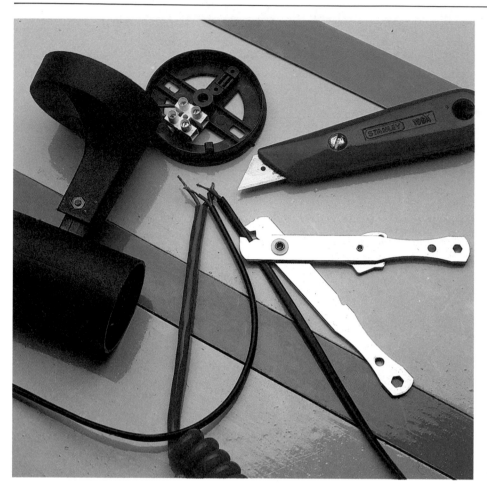

The two most important things to understand about home electrics are the technical terminology used to describe the electricity itself, and the nature of the system which is actually installed in your home.

Volts, amps and watts

Try to think of electricity in a wire as water in a pipe. The water must be under pressure or it will not flow. In electrical terms this pressure is known as the **voltage** and is measured in **volts**. The higher the pressure —or voltage—the harder the electricity is 'pushed' along the wire. In the UK, domestic electrical systems operate at 240 volts. This gives enough 'push' to get the electricity right around the house and through to any of your appliances.

Going back to the water pipe, it would be possible to measure how much water is flowing through it. In the same way you can measure how much electricity is flowing along a wire. This measurement is called the current and is measured in **amperes**, or **amps** for short. How big the current is depends on two factors. In a water system these would be the pressure and the size of the pipe. In the same way the size of an electric current depends on the voltage and what it is flowing through. This is why

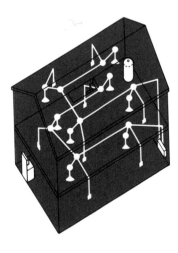

In older junction box lighting circuits the cable runs from the fuse board to junction boxes above the ceiling. Separate cables run to the ceiling roses and switches.

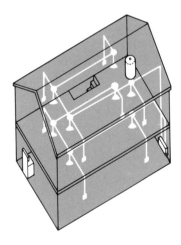

In a modern loop-in system the wiring is continuous, running from the fuse board to each ceiling rose in turn. The switches are wired directly to the roses, which act as junction boxes.

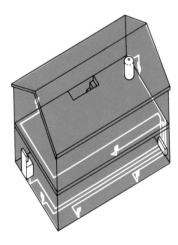

In older UK houses, a radial system runs separately from the main switch to each wall socket. There may be three or four fuse boxes connected to the meter with more than one main switch.

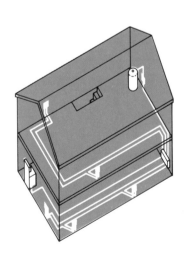

UK houses wired since 1947 use a ring main system with the power running from the consumer unit to each wall socket and back again. There is usually only one fuse board and one main switch

wires and appliances have a current rating —to tell you how much electricity can safely flow through them.

It is the size of the current that can make electricity dangerous, which is why you can still get a nasty shock from a car battery rated at only 12 volts. For a given voltage, it is also the current capacity which determines how much work an appliance can do —a kettle with a bigger element will boil the water faster. This capacity for work is measured in **watts** and takes into account both voltage and current by multiplying them together. So a 240 volt, 5 amp appliance consumes 240×5, or 1,200 watts. Working backwards, you can also find out that a 240 volt, 720 watt appliance will have a current rating of 3 amps. (1,000 watts is 1 kilowatt, 1 kW for short.)

Domestic electrical systems

Before the Second World War, British houses were wired on the radial system. Houses wired since 1947 employ a ring main. In the radial system all outlets—lights and sockets—are wired separately on circuits of various current ratings. Normally the wiring goes direct to a central point—the fuse board—but often one outlet is wired off another one for convenience. If the system has been abused, long spidery chains of outlets will have built up, each demanding more current than the wiring connecting them can safely handle.

In the ring system, the sockets on each floor of the house are connected by a separate 'ring' of wiring with a single current rating—normally 13 amps. The 'ring' starts at the consumer unit—the modern version of the fuse board—and then passes through each socket in turn before returning to the unit again. The lights in the house have their own separate radial circuit, and appliances demanding large amounts of current—cookers, showers, water heaters—are each wired direct to the consumer unit. This is also the case on radial-type circuits.

Wiring

The wiring is done with **cable**. Cable consists of a red insulated live wire, a black insulated neutral wire and a bare earth wire —all encased in a thick outer sheathing. Until the immediate post-war years this sheathing was rubber which has a safe life of only 25 years, after which time it starts to

perish. If this happens the current-carrying wires may touch and there is a serious risk of fire. So if you find any such cable in your system today, it must be replaced immediately.

The tough PVC sheathing that has replaced rubber lasts much longer—round about 70 years—but not indefinitely. Most authorities recommend that modern cable installations should be tested for deterioration every five to ten years and that most houses need to be completely rewired every 30 to 40 years.

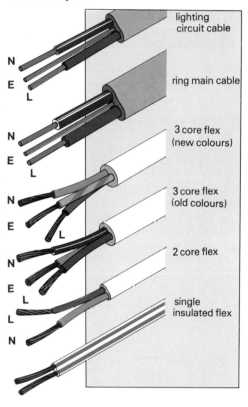

Cable is semi-rigid and carries electrical current in circuits. Flex (short for flexible conductor) carries the current from a socket via a plug to an appliance.

Finding out which system you have

The difference between radial and ring circuits may not be immediately obvious. The sockets originally installed with radial circuits were those of the round pinned types and had different current ratings— normally 10 amp, 5 amp and 2 amp. But in many cases these will have been replaced with the square pin type, found on all ring circuits, in the course of partially updating the system. So the place to start your investigation will be at the fuse board.

Ring circuit consumer units have the

fuses neatly in a row, each one guarding a separate circuit. In a typical two storey house there will be two socket ring circuits, for upstairs and downstairs, a lighting circuit, one to two spurs for larger appliances and one or two spare 'fuseways'. These are gaps to allow for the addition of new circuits.

Radial circuit fuse boards (which may be boxed) are by contrast confusing. It is very likely that there will be more than one board and they may all look very different. However, the number of cables running from them should give the game away.

The only way to be certain which system you have is to examine the socket wiring. Start by turning off the electricity at the main switch. Then unscrew the faceplates of at least three sockets around the house and examine the wires running into them.

Sockets wired on a ring main will have two sets of three wires. Each set will have a red live, a black neutral and an earth. The earth wire, which runs bare in the cable supplying the socket, should be insulated locally at the socket with a length of green and yellow PVC sheathing.

Sockets wired radially **should** have only one set of wires, however, you may be unlucky enough to choose a socket which is an extra socket itself or a power source for somewhere else. So you should continue opening up sockets until you have established a definite pattern and are certain which system you have.

Safety

Electricity, if not controlled, can pose a real danger and many household fires are a direct result of faulty installations. To cut down the worst risks, two safety measures are incorporated into the wiring—fuses and an earth.

A fuse is a deliberate weak link introduced into the live wire of an electrical circuit. Older-type fuses are simply lengths of thin wire fitted on to a porcelain body. Modern fuses enclose the wire inside a sealed cartridge to make replacement easier. If, for any reason, too much current flows through the fused circuit, the thin wire will melt, or 'blow', and shut off the current. Without a fuse the current would continue to flow until the circuit overheated and burnt out.

The house wiring system actually has a number of fuses to protect individual circuits. The whole house is protected by a **service fuse** fitted in a sealed box close to the meter. This is the responsibility of the Electricity board and cannot be repaired or replaced by the householder. However, it is only in exceptional circumstances that the service fuse will blow since each circuit has its own individual fuse which will almost certainly blow first if a fault develops.

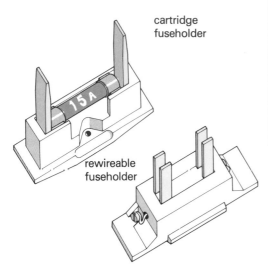

cartridge fuseholder

rewireable fuseholder

Fuse wire may be encased in a replaceable cartridge or run through a tube in the holder

Recognizing the individual fuses

Fuses are fitted in the consumer unit (or fuse board in older installations). Each circuit has its own fuse which is matched to the current rating of the circuit it is fitted in. Modern fuses and fuse carriers are colour coded: 5 amp is white (for lighting); 15 amp is blue (for immersion heaters and other 3 kW circuits); 20 amp is yellow (for some types of shower heater); 30 amp is red (power ring circuit) and 45 amp is green (for cookers). Old-style porcelain carriers have the current rating written on them and must be rewired with a correctly rated wire.

Alternatives to the conventional fuse

Some of the newer electrical installations have miniature circuit breakers (MCBs). These look like ordinary switches or push buttons but instead of blowing in the event of a fault, MCBs 'trip' and switch off the supply. Once the fault has been repaired, the circuit can be brought back into use simply by pressing the switch or button to reset it, thus eliminating the need to replace the fuse. Like fuses, MCB's are current rated for different circuits.

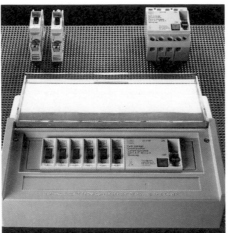

A modern consumer unit uses miniature circuit breakers instead of fuses

Protecting appliances

In modern installations the flexes to each appliance are also protected by their own fuses. These are fitted inside the plug, or spur connector for fixed appliances. They are always cartridge fuses and are current rated at either 3 amp (coloured red) or 13 amp (coloured brown). You may also find older 1 amp and 5 amp fuses. It is these fuses which will blow if anything goes wrong with an appliance or its flex—the most frequent cause of trouble. Older round-pin plugs do not have them, which in itself is a major reason for replacing them.

Earth wires

The purpose of an earth wire is to provide an escape path for the electricity—which quite literally runs back down this wire into the earth in the event of a fault. Though fuses protect the wiring from burning out, the earth wire directly protects **you**.

Some types of electrical faults on an appliance can make touchable parts live—for instance if an uninsulated wire is dropped onto a metal case. The earth wire is connected to the casing, so that if this were to happen, the electricity would instantly flow away down it. The large 'fault' current that this creates will blow the fuse, shutting off the supply and telling you that there is a fault. Earth terminals in an appliance are identified by the letter E, or sometimes by the symbol.

If you have old equipment with no earth wire it may be potentially dangerous. If you are at all uncertain you should have the appliance checked. But some modern equipment is designed not to need an earth. Its safety comes instead from **double insulation**, which means there is no possible way for a fault to put you in contact with live parts. Such equipment will be clearly marked DOUBLE INSULATED, or will carry the symbol ⊡ on the rating plate.

Electric shocks

If all your appliances and circuits are **properly** earthed or double-insulated, you should not get a shock even in the event of a fault. But if the earth is poor—perhaps because a contact is not secure—it is still possible that a lethal current could flow to earth through you. And there are some circumstances—for instance, if you drill through a buried cable and touch the chuck—where even a sound earth may not protect you.

Such possibilities are rare, but you can be protected against them if earth leakage circuit breakers (ELCBs, or sometimes called RCDs) are fitted to the circuit. These react very quickly to the leakage of any current to earth—quicker than the current can harm you—and shut off the supply. They are also very sensitive, and will trip if even a tiny current is detected. A fuse or MCB needs a fairly substantial current to cause it to trip, and this might well be enough to cause a fatal shock.

An ELCB can be wired to protect the whole installation—either fitted between the meter and the main switch, or used to replace the main switch entirely when it doubles as the main isolating switch. Individual ELCBs can also be installed to protect a single circuit or appliance. You can get sockets which incorporate them, and also portable, plug-in versions.

However, an ELCB should be regarded as a back-up device and is no substitute for ensuring that your installation or appliances are properly earthed in the first place.

CABLE AND FLEX

Electricity flows easily through certain materials—these are called conductors. Other substances—insulators—will block its progress. These two simple facts can be harnessed to control the flow of electricity around your home and direct it so that it goes where it is wanted.

Domestic wiring consists of a good conductor—usually copper—which carries the electricity around, surrounded by an insulator to contain it. Pages 4–6 give more details of the wiring system in general. But all household wiring is not the same. Different types of wiring are suitable for different types of circuit. One major division is between flex and cable, but within each category are many types.

The difference between flex and cable

Flex and cable are terms which are often confused and yet there is a very precise difference. Both consist of a number of insulated conductors colour coded for classification—and both carry electricity from A to B. But flex, as its name suggests, is a flexible cord. Cable on the other hand is semi-rigid; although it can easily be bent by hand, it will take up a set unless bent again.

Broadly speaking, cable is used for the permanent, fixed wiring which carries the electricity around the house to sockets, ceiling roses and fixed appliances like wall heaters. Flex is used for the final connection between a piece of electrical equipment and its plug, or a light fitting and its rose.

Colour codes for flex and cable

Since 1969 flex has had brown insulation for its live conductor, blue for the neutral and green and yellow for the earth if there is one. Cable is different: red insulation covers the live conductor and black covers the neutral (the only exception is three core and earth cable or strapping wire which is used for two way switching—for a light on the stairs for example. The conductors are insulated in red, blue and yellow, but only for purposes of identification). The earth is bare inside the sheath, but should be covered with a sleeve of green and yellow insulation wherever the sheath is stripped

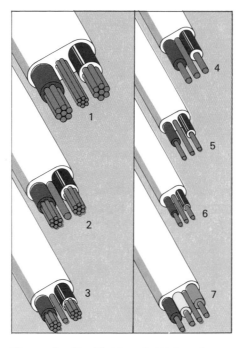

Types of cable: (1) 10mm². (2) 6mm². (3) 4mm². (4) 2.5mm². (5) 1.5mm². (6) 1mm². (7) 1mm² three core and earth cable

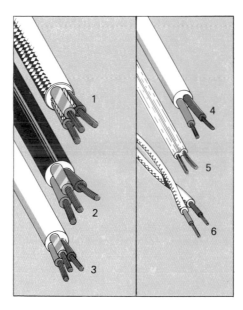

Types of flex: (1) Unkinkable. (2) Rubber sheathed. (3) 1.5mm² PVC sheathed three core. (4) 0.75mm² PVC sheathed two core. (5) Parallel twin flex. (6) Twisted flex

back to make a connection—inside a socket or ceiling rose for example. The earth is a safety device. It carries current only when a fault develops in the circuit. If this happens the fuse protecting the circuit blows and for the short time that current flows along the earth conductor, the outer sheathing of the cable is sufficient protection.

Cable for lighting circuits and sockets

The cable commonly used for all modern house circuits is called **twin and earth**. This is PVC-sheathed cable containing two PVC insulated cores with a bare earth. Twin and earth cable has a flat rather than round cross section—a feature of electric cable which is unique to the UK but does have the advantage of being neater for surface wiring. You'll find that the only difference between the cable used for a lighting circuit and the cable used for a circuit supplying electricity to your sockets is in the actual size.

The size of a cable is measured by the thickness of its cores and is given as the cross-sectional area of a core in square millimetres—for example, 1.00m² cable is commonly used for lighting circuits. The size of cable—and flex—is important because it determines the amount of electric current that can be carried. If a cable is too small for the current it has to carry, it will overheat, melt the insulation and expose the metal core. This can result in fire—around 3,000 fires a year in the UK (6 per cent of all domestic fires) are caused by faults in the permanent wiring.

The power sockets in a house are usually connected to a cable which runs from a fuse in the fuse-box around the sockets and back to the fuse again. This is a ring-circuit. The circuit is normally run in 2.5mm² cable and is protected by a 30 amp fuse. In every house there are also special circuits which draw a lot of current. These are best wired with their own cable from a separate fuse. The size of cable depends on the equipment.

Choosing flex

As flex is used for connecting electrical equipment you'll generally have a particular appliance in mind when you come to buy it. The most important thing you need to know is whether the equipment needs to be connected to earth. Appliances like irons and electric heaters and such things as metal light fittings always do, but nowadays a lot of equipment has a double protection of insulation and does not need an earth connection. You'll find that such appliances—hair driers, lawnmowers and electric drills for example—will be clearly marked or will carry the double insulation symbol ⊒ .

You will also need to know how much current the equipment will draw as this determines the size of the flex. And it is worth considering whether there are any special conditions which might point towards a special type of flex.

Different types of flex

There are two core and three core flexes: the first for double insulated equipment, the second for appliances that require an earth. Two core flex is usually round sheathed with colour coded connectors, but there are also thinner twin flexes which are sometimes used for light fittings. There is a parallel and a twist type—neither has colour coding so care is needed to identify the conductors.

Three-core flex is always round sheathed with colour coded conductors. As well as the ordinary PVC types there are three main other types—heat resistant for storage heaters and immersion heaters, unkinkable for irons, and tough-rubber-sheathed (TRS) for lawnmowers and other equipment whose flex may be subject to rough treatment. This type of flex is often sheathed orange but you should not assume that this is always so.

It is vital to choose flex with the right number of cores. Always use three core if there is an earth and note that extension leads should always be made from three-core flex. This is because you cannot guarantee that an extension lead will never be used with a piece of equipment which needs to be earthed.

Other types of wire

Coaxial cable is a strange type of wire—not strictly a cable since it is flexible—used only for connecting television aerials or, in the thinner gauges, for hi-fi systems. It has a central copper core surrounded by sheathing designed to cut out interference with the television or audio signal. Another type is bell wire—more properly called extra low voltage wire. This is used to connect things like door bells which run on a very low voltage supplied either from a battery or

from the mains via a transformer which reduces your voltage supply from 240V to around 12 volts or even less.

There is one other cable you may come across—called mineral insulated copper sheathed (MICS). This is used for outside circuits and very occasionally indoors. Using MICS is something you should not attempt until you have considerable experience with wiring, and even then you may think twice. The mineral insulation surrounding the copper cores absorbs water so the ends of the cable must be sealed.

Getting the right size

In most parts of the UK the voltage is 240V so you can reckon that for every 1,000W a piece of equipment will draw you are going to need a flex current capacity of 4 amps.

Remember the larger the size of cable or flex that you buy, the greater its current carrying capacity and the higher its cost. But don't skimp as your safety is at risk.

The current carrying capacities of the most common sizes of flex and cable are:

mm^2	0.5	0.75	1.0	1.25	1.5	2.5	4
Amps	3	6	10	13	15	20	25

Always buy the next size up to the one you actually need.

Note that with pendant flexes for ceiling lights you also need to think about the weight the flex will have to carry—a 3 amp flex can support 2kg, a 10 amp flex can support 3kg and larger flexes 5kg.

When choosing cable you will find that most of the circuits in a house are run in one or two sizes—$1.0mm^2$ for lighting and $2.5mm^2$ for ring circuits. It is only for fixed appliances that you'll need thicker cable.

Apart from choosing the right size and type, you should make sure that all the connections are well made with only as much insulation and sheathing stripped off as is necessary. You should also avoid tight bends when installing cable and you should unravel flex before you use it. Make sure that the flex is properly anchored at both ends—in the plug and to the piece of equipment it supplies.

Tools for handling flex and cable

A minimum of tools are necessary—just a trimming knife for stripping the sheath and insulation and a screwdriver for making the connections. However, there are two other tools which are handy and will help you to

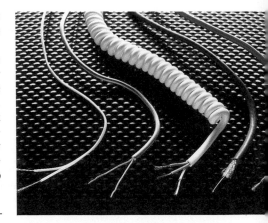

Other types of wire (from left to right) include bell wire, MICS, coiled flex, coaxial and orange tough rubber sheathed

do a more professional job—a pair of strippers and a pair of long nosed pliers.

The wire strippers strip both cable and flex much more quickly than a knife and can be set so that the copper cores are not damaged in the process. The long nosed pliers help to bend the cores at the end when making the connections—this is most useful with larger cables whose large cores can be well-nigh impossible to bend with your bare fingers.

Cable or flex exposed on the surface of a wall can be held to the surface with wrap-around clips called buckle clips—these have the advantage that they can easily be undone—or with the better looking plastic hoop and pin type of clip. They should be spaced every 300mm or so. Surface cables can also be run in plastic channelling which protects the cable as well as securing it.

Stripping cable

To strip cable slit the outer sheath lengthways with a sharp penknife or trimming knife. Don't cut back too much —about 75mm should be adequate. Peel back the sheathing like the skin of a banana and cut off the waste.

The best way to strip the live and neutral wires is with a wire stripper—a cheap, easy-to-use tool you can buy from any DIY store. At a pinch, you could cut around the insulation with a knife; but take extra care not to nick the wires. Don't use pliers—they are too difficult to control accurately.

Adjust the wire stripper until the blade just begins to cut through the insulation; then pull gently towards the wire ending so that the insulation is removed and a length of the inner core exposed. Trim back about 20mm on both the live and neutral wires.

FIXING FUSES

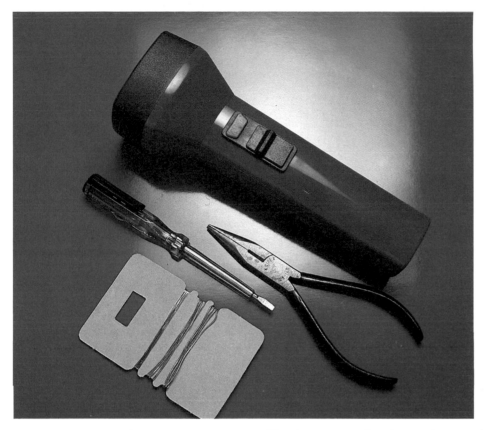

Domestic electrical fuses are deliberate weak links in the system, designed to break when a fault occurs. Electrical faults take many different forms and can occur almost anywhere in the wiring, but most have one thing in common: they cause an abnormally large amount of current to flow in the adjacent flex or cable.

Simple fuses are wires combining high resistance—which means they heat up fast —with a low melting point. So when an abnormal current flows through a high-resistance fuse, the fuse melts and breaks the circuit. Current is measured in amps, which is also what fuses are rated in. Consequently a 5 amp fuse would melt if a current of 13 amps were passed through it; a 13 amp fuse would not.

In Britain, household fuse systems are designed to provide several lines of defence which protect both you and the electrical hardware. The two main weapons in this system are the fuses themselves, which halt a dangerous build-up of current—and the earthing system which disposes of it safely.

Although some appliances have their own built-in fuse, the first line of defence is generally the cartridge fuse that is found in the plug.

Plug fuses are rated at 3 amps for small appliances consuming under 750 watts— toasters, hi-fi and lamps for example—and 13 amps for over-750 watt appliances, like fires, kettles, televisions and videos. Confusingly, other ratings of fuse are available (such as 5 amp), but they are not required for home use.

Most people happily operate small appliances on a 13 amp plug fuse—happily, that is, until the appliance fails. Although it's not really dangerous to do so, it does make sense to give your equipment as much protection as possible—especially when it comes so cheaply in the form of a fuse.

As well as being fitted in plugs, plug fuses are also found in fused connection units— the fixed sockets used to supply kitchen appliances, wall heaters and the like.

After that comes the circuit fuse — they're the ones you'll find in a row in your fuse box or consumer unit. Each lighting and socket circuit in the house has a circuit fuse and there are additional ones for the individual circuits supplying high power equipment such as the cooker and immersion heater.

Circuit fuses are rated according to the current flowing in the electrical circuit which they are protecting:
- Lighting circuits are 5 amps.
- Socket (power) circuits are 15 amps.
- Small cooker, shower and immersion heater circuits are 20 amps.
- Large cooker, shower and immersion heater circuits are 30 or 45 amps.

Conventional fuses can be of two types. Older, rewireable fuses consist of a thin strand of fuse wire running between the terminals of the fuse holder. The wire is current-rated according to the list above.

Newer fuses have a cartridge similar to a plug fuse, only larger—easier to replace than rewireable fuses, but you can't quickly tell if they've blown.

Both these types have their fuse holders colour coded:
- White—5 amp.
- Blue—15 amp.
- Yellow—20 amp.
- Red—30 amp.
- Green—45 amp.

In more sophisticated modern consumer units miniature circuit breakers (MCBs) are fitted instead of fuses.

What causes fuses to blow

It's essential to know what can cause the current build-up that eventually melts a fuse before you set about faultfinding.

Short circuit: This is the classic electrical fault. It means, quite simply, that the outgoing live current is allowed to run straight into the returning neutral current, bypassing the appliance in the process. This allows a massive flow of current.

Short circuits are usually caused by faulty connections or by deterioration in the wiring, though outside factors such as dampness or a stray drill bit can have the same effect.

Insulation failure: Though poor insulation can create a short circuit, an insulation failure within an appliance may result in part or all of it becoming live. This causes a current build-up which the fuse should halt, before you get a shock.

Poor connections: When a connection becomes weak or loose, it may cause the current to surge across it; fuses respond to this and blow accordingly.

Appliance failure: If the electrical circuitry in an appliance breaks down—say, when the element of an electric kettle fails—the impedance of that appliance falls

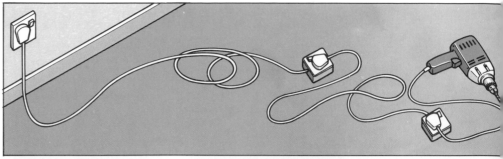

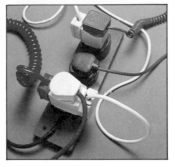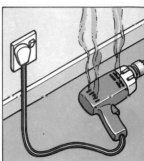

to a low level. The result is very similar to a short circuit: a current build-up, then a blown fuse.

Over-extensions: Electric cable and flex sizes are carefully determined not only by the amount of electrical current they can handle but also by how far they can carry it. Consequently, overlong flexes and extension leads, or circuits which extend further than the guidelines laid down by the IEE can result in current surges which blow fuses—sometimes after many years of trouble-free service.

Overloading: This is perhaps the most common cause of blown fuses. When an electrical wire is asked to carry more current than it can handle it heats up. Hopefully, as they are designed this way, the wire that heats up fastest is the fuse.

It is a common fallacy to suppose that just because a 15 amp power circuit can supply several sockets, so a single socket should, via an adaptor, be able to supply two or even three appliances. Often, the socket connections, adaptor and plugs simply cannot handle all that is asked of them. They heat up, the insulation begins to break down and the circuit fuse blows.

Before a fuse blows

You can save yourself a lot of trouble later by taking two simple measures as soon as you move into a property.

First turn off the main switch at the consumer unit and remove all the fuse holders but one (on MCBs press the small 'off' button below the reset button).

Turn on the electricity and note what lights, sockets or appliances are served by the fuse that you've left. Note the information down and stick it to the fuseholder. Then check that the fuse's colour coding is correct.

Repeat this procedure for each fuse in turn, always remembering to shut off the main switch between times. Once you have circuit information on all the fuse holders you won't be in the dark if a fuse blows.

Secondly, make sure that you have fuse wire or cartridges (as applicable), a screwdriver, pliers and torch in a handy place near the consumer unit. Rummaging around in the dark can be dangerous.

Faultfinding—plug fuse

If an appliance goes dead but none of the others fed from sockets on the same circuit are affected, suspect a blown plug fuse.

Blown plug fuses are caused by a variety of reasons: among them are using too many extension leads (top); overloading a single wall socket by abusing a multi-

1. If you have not already done so switch off before opening up the plug. The fuse may look charred, or it may not—but in any case you must check the appliance, the flex and the plug for faults before fitting a new one.

First of all check the rating of the fuse—and then the wattage of the appliance. If the former is only 3 amps and the latter is over 750 watts, you've found the fault.
2. Follow on by looking at the plug connections: they should all be tight and there should be no stray strands that could short from one to another.

Check the plug in the socket. If it is a loose fit, one or the other may be badly worn and in need of replacement.

Move on to the flex. It should be tightly held in the plug's cord grip. Along its

adaptor (left), accidentally knocking fluid over an electrical appliance (centre) or by plugging a faulty appliance into the circuit and then switching on

length there should be no evidence of fraying, splitting, kinking or twisting—any of which may cause a blown fuse.
3. Finally, check the appliance. Start with where the flex enters it—the rubber grommet should be intact and there should be no appreciable movement when you pull it. If there is, this indicates loose terminals or cord grips inside.

Often, misuse or maltreatment of an appliance can blow a fuse. For example, an excessive buildup of dust or dirt can cause overheating, and the same problem results from restricting the airflow around it— particularly on hi-fis and videos. Foreign objects, too, cause problems and bear in mind that something may have fallen in accidentally.

Charring indicates a blown fuse—first check the rating. Too much bare wire plus stray strands may cause shorting.

Worn grommets often lead to damaged flex insulation. You need to replace both the flex and the grommet.

1 *Too many spurs from one socket will overload the circuit*

2 *Cracks in sockets are a tell-tale sign of trouble within*

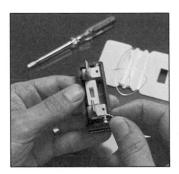

3 *Make sure that the fuse wire is of the correct rating*

4 *Check pendant light fittings for loose wires and reconnect*

Faultfinding—circuit fuses

With a bit of luck, your observations at the time the fuse blows should give you more than an inkling as to where the trouble lies—more often than not it happens when you switch something on.

For this reason, and hopefully to save you having to conduct a systematic survey of your house's electrical system, the checks below are grouped according to the most common individual trouble spots.

Overloading: If a socket is overloaded, you'll almost certainly recognise the fault as soon as it happens. Three-way adaptors (which do have their own plug-type fuse) are a particularly common source of trouble and their use should be avoided.

If you must have a three-way adaptor, make sure you never run high-power appliances—such as a kettle—from it.

Circuit overloading is harder to recognise, but it can easily happen if you have all your high-power appliances—washing machine, spin drier, TV, fan heater, kettle—running at the same time. If the problem recurs frequently, have the circuit checked by a qualified electrician.

Appliance failure: Serious faults within an appliance can cause a circuit fuse to blow as well as the plug or connection unit fuse.

Light switches: In the case of a suspect switch, turn off the mains electricity.

Remove the switch faceplate and inspect the connections behind. The red and black wires should be held tight in their terminals—with no stray strands to cause short circuits—and the insulation should be complete, without nicks.

Now look at the earth wire. This should be attached to a terminal on the switch box and covered with a length of green and yellow plastic sheathing. A loose earth terminal means the switch may not be properly earthed: a bare earth wire can cause a short circuit.

Sockets: These suffer from more or less the same problems as light switches—loose connections or shorting via an uninsulated earth wire (in this case live, neutral and earth wires are held in terminals in the back of the socket faceplate).

Having made sure the electricity is turned off, unscrew the faceplate and make a thorough inspection.

Incorrect fuse rating: This may seem obvious, but it's a common fault. Even if the colour code on the fuse holder is correct, you should also check the cartridge. And if the fuses are rewireable don't assume that the blown wire was of the correct rating. Check the figure stamped on the fuse with the ratings on the fuse wire packet to make sure you use the right one.

Among the other faults to look out for are: cracking or worn terminals, in which case the socket must be replaced; kinking of the cable where it enters the backing box, in which case the cable must be pulled through and trimmed.

Light fittings: Turn off the electricity and remove the rose or the body of the fitting. Be on the lookout for loose wires, stray strands and perished or broken insulation.

Mending a fuse

Plug fuse: Simply open up the plug, flick out the old fuse with a screwdriver and slot the new one in. In the case of fused connection units, the fuseholder either unscrews or is prised out with a screwdriver. Slot in the new fuse and replace.

Circuit fuse (cartridge): Remove the fuseholder of the circuit that has failed. Dig out the old fuse and slot in its replacement.

Circuit fuse (rewireable): These may be one of several patterns, notably open or enclosed, but the principles are the same.

Remove the relevant fuseholder and loosen the screw terminals at either end to release any burnt wire.

Cut off sufficient new wire of the correct rating to stretch the length of the holder and wrap around the terminals.

Wrap one end clockwise round one of the terminals and tighten. Feed the wire across or through the holder as necessary.

Wrap the other end round the other terminal—again in a clockwise direction—and tighten. Replace the fuseholder.

MCBs and ELCBs: Simply press the reset button once the fault has been put right.

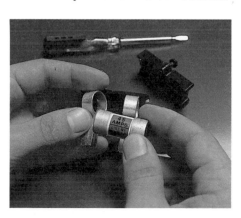

5 *Make sure you use the correct rating of cartridge fuse*

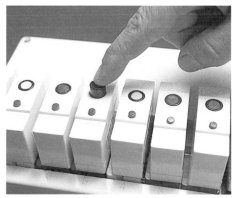

6 *Only reset a circuit breaker after correcting the fault*

CHAPTER 2

LIGHTS AND SWITCHES

Some of the most common electrical jobs are often the easiest to tackle. Broken or faulty light switches can usually be repaired quickly and easily providing you track down the source of the problem. And fitting a dimmer switch is a straightforward task that need take no longer than half an hour. Even fitting a new ceiling light is not a difficult job, if you tackle the work systematically

REPAIRING LIGHT FITTINGS

A fluorescent light should operate without trouble for thousands of hours. And after it's been working normally, it's very unlikely that it will suddenly fail completely to come on. If a fault does occur, look at the tube, because the way this reacts will point you to where the problem lies. Remember, it doesn't have to be with the tube, it's often with the starter. The starter is a small drum-shaped device which is usually fitted to the side of the tube.

Recognising starter failure: First make the basic check of inspecting the fitting to confirm that it is a switch starter type and not a quick start tube which doesn't need a starter—a typical starter model is shown in the illustration. Then turn on the light and watch the ends of the tube. If both elements glow white but the tube doesn't light you've got a faulty starter which will need to be replaced. But don't confuse this with only one element glowing, as this indicates a fault with the respective lampholder. Similarly, if the tube flickers, or if it comes on and then goes off every few seconds, the problem is likely the starter. But a very old

tube can sometimes show these symptoms.

If you think you've identified a fault with the starter, it'll need to be replaced, as it can't be repaired. The starter socket is often located inconspicuously on the side of the casing towards one end. This enables you to remove it without having to take out the diffuser or the tube. On some small types of fluorescents, though, you may find that you have to remove these in order to gain access to the starter.

Push the starter in slightly and then rotate it anticlockwise so that it is free to be lifted out. Replace it with one of exactly the same type. The commonest kind is a two-pin 'glow' starter. Insert the new unit, push it fully home and then rotate it clockwise to lock it in position.

Replacing an old flex

The procedures for replacing the flex on a standard lamp, table or desk light are virtually the same. They may have to be modified slightly depending on the design of the light.

Usually the flex is concealed within the fitting and has an outlet point on the side near the bottom so that base of the light can stand flat on the table or floor. Sometimes a standard lamp has feet so the flex can be taken under the base and then up the central column to the lampholder at the top. With a desk lamp, the lampholder and switch mechanism are fixed to a bracket which in turn is fixed to the metal cone

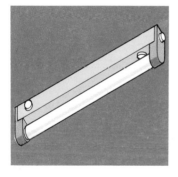
5 *Starters may be located at various points on the light fitting*

2 *To remove the starter push it in slightly and rotate it*

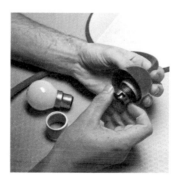
3 *Take out the bulb and then gently ease down the lampholder*

4 *With a screwdriver unscrew the terminals to release the flex cores*

5 *Tie a string to the old flex before you draw it out, as shown here*

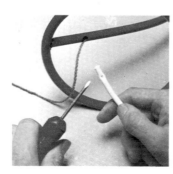
6 *Pierce a small hole in the end of the new flex and thread the string through it*

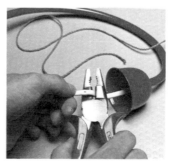
7 *Draw the new flex up through the fitting, then cut off the damaged end*

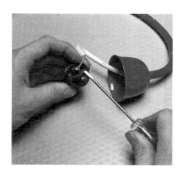
8 *Secure the new cores to the lampholder and reassemble the lamp*

shade with self-tapping screws.

To remove the old flex, take out the bulb and take off the lampshade or cover. On table and standard lamps this is held in place by a screw-down ring or the skirt of the lampholder. On desk lamps unscrew the bracket from the cone and then ease down the lampholder so the flex connections are exposed. Unscrew the terminals to free the cores from the lampholder.

With standard and table lamps you need to unscrew the top half of the lampholder to get to the terminals. Do this by holding the

---

★ WATCH POINT ★

Use a bradawl to pierce a small hole through the flex very near to one end. Thread the draw wire or string through the hole and tie it back on itself. This makes a more secure fixing than if you just tied the wire or string round the top. It also means that the flex is less likely to catch as it is drawn round any bends which occur along its path.

---

flex you should upgrade this anyway. As a general rule, if the lamp has any exposed metal parts then it should be earthed.

Draw the new flex up through the light fitting using a draw wire.

On some lamps a draw wire may not be necessary and the 'stiffness' in the flex may be sufficient for it to be pushed through the base unit. And on some china lamp bases you may be able to remove the felt pad from the bottom so you can get your hand inside to feed up the flex to the lampholder.

5. Once the flex has been drawn through, cut off the end beyond the hole to release the draw wire. The insulation on the flex cores in all probability will have been damaged by the bradawl so this section must be discarded.

6. Next, prepare the ends using the old flex as a guide for the amount of insulation and sheathing to remove. Then secure the cores, including the earth, to the terminals. However, before doing this it's worth checking to see if the cores need heat-resisting sleeving.

Now screw the terminal housing and cover back together. With table and standard lamps, you may once again find it

---

push the cap of the bulb against the spring pins in the lampholder, rotate it to clear the fixing cups and then pull it free.

First, turn off the light switch and the power to the circuit. If there is sufficient glass left you may still be able to take out the bulb as you would do normally. But wear a thick gardening glove, and grip the bulb as near to the base as possible.

Unscrew the skirt from round the socket to expose enough of the metal cap of the bulb for you to grip in a gloved hand. If this proves awkward, push pliers into the end of the cap to depress and rotate it. Open the jaws a little as you do this so the outside edges of the pliers make contact with the inside of the cap.

★ WATCH POINT ★

Alternatively, cover the broken bulb with a **thick** polythene bag and tap away the remaining glass, including the centre spindle carrying the filaments. The bag will stop splinters flying into the air.

9 *If you can get a grip, use a glove to protect your hand*

10 *Use pliers to grip the base of the broken bulb*

11 *Hold the fuse against the casing and the battery*

12 *Hold the bowl with one hand and undo the screws*

---

top half and rotating the bottom section attached to the base unit. You may find it easier doing it this way round because the flex won't twist and kink as much as you are working.

Once the flex is free, you should be able to draw it back through the unit. But before you do this, tie some string or thin wire to the end of one of the flex cores so that it can be pulled through the lamp as the old flex is removed and then used to draw the new flex into the lamp.

Measure out the length of new flex you need. This may be two- or three-core depending on whether the lamp needs to be earthed. If the light has the original flex then use this as a guide—although with very old lights that have obsolete types of

easier to rotate the base rather than the socket to prevent kinking the flex. Then fit the shade and the skirt that prevents you from touching metal parts of the socket while you're changing a bulb. On desk lamps you may have to fit the skirt before attaching the headgear to a bracket which in turn is screwed inside the metal shade.

At the other end of the flex fit a three-pin plug with a **3 amp** fuse (colour-coded red).

Removing a broken bulb

How you go about this job depends on how much of the bulb is broken and the type of socket it is fitted to. So be prepared to improvize. Basically, what you have to do is

---

Testing a plug fuse

If you are unsure whether a fuse in a plug has blown or the appliance it serves is at fault, you can check the fuse using a metal-cased torch.

First switch on to check that the torch is working. Then hold the torch upside down and unscrew the bottom cap to expose the base of the batteries. Put the torch in the on position and hold the fuse so that one end touches the battery and the other the metal casing. If the torch lights (i.e., the fuse completes the circuit), you'll know that the fuse is in working order. You will then need to look elsewhere for the fault: first recheck the flex and bulb as shown above.

Bowl light fittings

There are various types of bowl light fittings which fully, or partially, encompass the light bulb.

Many modern decorative bowl fittings are suspended from a single chain. To release the bowl look for the screws on the side of the metal cup into which the rim is inserted. When done up, these screws locate under the lip of the rim. Undoing them will allow the bowl to drop down. The procedure is trickier than it sounds because you need one hand to support the bowl and the other to turn the screws. So there's no free hand to steady yourself, say, if you're working over a stairwell. Therefore, slacken all the screws first with a screwdriver, so you can undo them fully later with your fingers.

Another type of fitting also encloses the bulb, but can be close mounted either to a wall or, more usually, on a ceiling.

There are some elaborate fixings which invisibly hold the bowl in place. One type, for example, has a metal backplate which acts as a base for the lampholder. The bowl

Fitting a torpedo switch

Most table, desk and standard lamps incorporate a switch in the lampholder. But access to the switch could be awkward. The neat answer to the problem is to fit a slimline torpedo switch.

With the plug removed and by your side, unscrew the cover and hold the torpedo switch against the flex in the exact place you want to fit it. Mark the position of the cord clamps on the flex with insulation tape and cut a 'window' in the flex as shown. Take extra care that you don't cut through the core insulation.

Using the switch as a guide, cut the live (brown) core and possibly the blue (neutral) core—this depends on the design of the switch—so they will fit into their respective terminals.

Note that the switch is wired into the live core, so connect the brown cores to the two terminals on the switch housing. The blue cores go to the terminals to one side of this. Usually, torpedo switches don't need to be earthed, so any earth core can run through unbroken. You can also leave the neutral

take off the diffuser, if one is fitted. Support the tube with one hand while easing back the spring-loaded end plate and socket with the other. This will free the tube from the socket. Lower it slightly to pull it from the other end. Fitting a new tube follows the reverse order.

Bayonet-type tubes: If you're replacing a tube which has a bayonet end fitting similar to an ordinary light bulb first pull back or remove the protective cover to reveal the sockets. Then push the tube into the spring-loaded holder at one end and rotate to free it. Do likewise at the other end. Push the new tube into the sockets first and then turn to secure. Finally fit the diffuser back in place.

Renewing a pull-switch cord

The easiest way of replacing a dirty or frayed cord is to cut it off near the switch and then use a plastic cord connector to join on a new length. Slip the cup of the connector over the stub of old cord and tie a knot so that it can't drop off. Similarly, slip the other section of the connector over the

13 *Cut a window in the flex at the point you have marked*

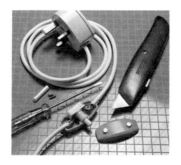

14 *Wire up the live core to the terminals and fit the cover*

15 *First remove the diffuser in order to gain access to the tube*

16 *Release the tube from the socket at one end and lift it down*

fits over the plate and then a lever is activated to move catches under the rim to keep it in place.

To remove the bowl, at ceiling level you should be able to see the slightly bent end of the recessed lever. Pull this out towards you. Push the bowl upwards to clear the catches then push the lever round to retract the catches leaving you free to lower the bowl to expose the bulb.

> ★ WATCH POINT ★
>
> If there's any risk of the bowl slipping free without warning, tape it securely to the fitting to stop it dropping.

uncut if you prefer and if there is room.

Screw on the cord clamps and the cover before testing.

Replacing a fluorescent tube

Before touching the tube make sure that the light has been turned off.

Bi-pin tube: This is now the most common type of tube. At each end there are two small pins which project from insulated caps. These pins locate in the sockets on the casing. As these are also well insulated it's virtually impossible to come into contact with a live connection.

To remove an old tube of this kind first

end of the new cord and again tie a knot. Then screw the two sections together to hold the cord in place.

If you wish to replace the cord entirely, then you'll have to dismantle the switch. First, turn off the light and the power to the circuit. Undo the faceplate and disconnect the circuit cable. This will free the switch.

Carefully undo the screws holding the switch mechanism to the back of the faceplate. You'll find that the cord is threaded up through two concentric springs, a metal contact plate and plastic cover. It is prevented from being pulled out by a knot which rests inside a plastic bush. Before dismantling this section make a sketch of it so you know the exact order in which to reassemble the bits and pieces.

FITTING DIMMER SWITCHES

The surprising thing about dimmer switches is not that they are now so popular but that they have taken so long to become readily available to the householder.

Different activities in the home call for different levels of light: low, reassuring levels in the nursery, soft light for watching TV, mood lighting for supper parties, and background light for specific tasks such as writing or sewing where you need a concentrated source.

The expensive solution is to have numerous lights, each one tailored to your needs. The low-cost answer is to fit dimmer switches and get more mileage from your pendant lights. And where your room has more than one light you can create an even level of light rather than having to make do with bright and dark patches in a room.

Because fitting dimmers creates lower levels of light using less electricity, it means that you can afford to leave hall and stairway lights on—an important safety feature—and time-delay dimmers make it possible to leave security lights on when you go out for the evening without burning a hole in your household budget.

Dimmer switches are easy to install. You simply turn off at the mains, take out your old switch, connect the dimmer to the existing wires and switch on. All you need is a screwdriver and perhaps a pair of pliers. It shouldn't take you much more than half an hour.

Buying a dimmer switch

The difficult part of installing a dimmer switch is deciding which one you want from the variety that are available. Almost all are designed as straight replacements for ordinary light switches. The most common type (featured here) has a square plastic cover plate with a rotary knob mounted in the middle; the on-off switch may be built into the control knob or separate.

But there are many variations. They come with decorative faceplates in different materials, and with pairs of knobs or sometimes none at all.

Some dimmers incorporate a separate on-off switch which allows you to set the level of lighting the day before; others have auto-matic on-off operation when the room starts to get dark. The control knob may be very large, or it may be set at 90° to act as an edge wheel control. Some switch plates glow in the dark. The more sophisticted dimmer switches consist simply of a plain or decorative plate which changes the level of light according to how long you touch it. Others of this type turn on and off when you tap the plate with a finger and yet others can be controlled remotely—from your arm-chair for example. Many dimmers have a facility for two-way wiring—such as on a landing light.

Fitting restrictions

There are a few restrictions to bear in mind when you go window shopping or look through the manufacturers' brochures. For example, if you have fluorescent lights you need to get a special fluorescent dimmer. Depending on the model you buy you may also have to make modifications to the lights themselves. These usually involve fitting a new ballast and an extra resistor to the switch circuit; unless you know about fluorescent lights it's probably easier to buy new lights, ready adapted.

If the switches you want to replace are the two-way type make sure that you specify that the dimmers are suitable for this appli-cation and can take the extra wire (the cable between two-way switches is three core and earth instead of the standard twin core and earth—see page 18).

If your switch plate has several switches in it there shouldn't be any problem. You can normally control several lights from one dimmer providing you do not exceed the dimmer's total wattage rating and can fit the wires safely in the terminals at the back.

On the other hand you may prefer to control each light separately. You can buy two-gang dimmers which have two control knobs on a standard square plate, and bigger switch plates with more control knobs are also available. But remember that unless you are prepared to cut a hole for a larger metal switch box in the wall you should buy a dimmer whose plate is the same size as your present conventional light switch.

It's important to check the depth of your present switch box. Some dimmers won't fit in shallow plaster-depth boxes, others are slimline fittings. Switch off the mains at the

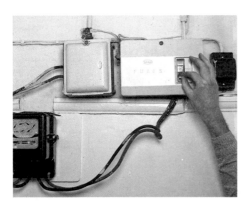

1 *Make absolutely sure that you shut off the main switch before opening the existing switch*

2 *Double check by testing the light before you unscrew the faceplate of the switch*

3 *With the switch opened, use a mains tester screwdriver to check again for live wires*

your dimmer, make sure its thickness (excluding the faceplate) doesn't exceed this depth.

4 *If the earth wire is bare, disconnect it and slip on a length of green and yellow sheathing*

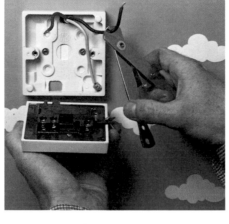

5 *Test fit the wires against the dimmer switch then trim them back and strip them as necessary*

Fitting a one-way dimmer

First of all switch off the house power supply at the main fuse board or consumer unit. The whole job shouldn't take you more than half an hour, so there's no danger of the fridge or freezer defrosting seriously. Electricity is dangerous so follow a strict safety procedure before you disconnect the existing light switch. Make sure that the switch you are about to replace really is disconnected by trying it. Then, with the switch safely isolated from the mains, unscrew the two screws on either side of the faceplate and gently pull it away from its mounting box. From now onwards check all the bare wires you come across with a mains tester screwdriver. You hold the bare blade of the insulated screwdriver against the bare wire and touch the plate built into the end. If the small neon in the handle lights up you have a live wire. Don't touch it until you've made sure that the main switch on the fuseboard really has been turned off.

Using a small screwdriver, unscrew the terminals to free the attached red and black wires from the back of the switch plate. It is likely that the copper earth wire is screwed to the metal box. There's no need to disconnect this unless it has been left bare. If it has, it's a good idea to sleeve the earth before you refit the switch (it cuts down the risk of short circuits in a crowded switch box). To this end, unscrew the terminal and remove the wire. Cut a length of green and yellow striped PVC sleeving to slip over the wire—leaving enough bare at the end to connect to the box terminal screw.

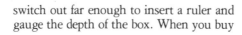

6 *Connect the mains feed and switch line wires to the terminals specified by the makers*

7 *On this example, you switch on and then vary the brightness via a separate rotary control*

fuse board or consumer unit and then unscrew the switch faceplate. Pull the

switch out far enough to insert a ruler and gauge the depth of the box. When you buy

Now check that the new dimmer switch fits comfortably in the backing box. If all is well, loosen the screws on the back of the switch and test-fit the wires. If the new terminals are less deep than those of the old switch, trim the wires so that the insulation butts up hard against the outside of the terminals with no bare wire visible.

When the wires have been trimmed correctly connect them to the switch. Always follow the maker's instructions about which terminals to use. In a one-way switch both the red and black cable covers are 'live' because the switch is simply a break in the live part of the lighting circuit. For the purposes of following the manufacturer's instructions treat the red wire as the 'feed' from the mains and the black wire (the switch line) as its extension to the light. As a reminder, put a short piece of red tape around the black wire to indicate that this too is live when the switch is on. Finally, screw the PVC sheathed earth wire to the backing box.

If you have bought a metal faced dimmer switch there will be an earth terminal on the back. Make sure that this is connected to the earth terminal on the metal box using an offcut of cable core. Like the cable earth wire, it's best to sheath it in green and yellow PVC sleeving.

Screw on the dimmer switch. The manufacturers will supply the screws and these should fit into the threaded adjustable lugs on the sides of the metal box without difficulty.

When the screws are almost home, adjust the switch plate so that it is square then tighten them up hard.

Faultfinding: Turn the switch off, rotating the knob anticlockwise until it clicks. Now turn on again at the mains and check that your new dimmer operates correctly. If it doesn't, go through this checklist below until you manage to track down the fault.

• Are your other lighting and power circuits working?
• Have you more than one main switch and have you switched them all on?
• If you have fuses has one of them blown?
• If you have miniature circuit breakers, has one of them been tripped off?

If the problem is clearly only with the circuit you have been working on, switch off at the mains again, following the same procedure as before, and unscrew the dimmer switch.

Check that the wires are tightly fixed in their correct terminals, that there are no loose wires in the box and that no bare wires can touch each other or (the earth wire excepted) the metal box.

Check that the back of the dimmer is not fouling a wire or that a screw or a sharp edge has not accidentally cut the insulation to wires. Replace, switch on at the mains and retest the switch.

Two-way and multi-gang dimmers

Two-way and multi-gang dimmers are fitted in exactly the same way as a simple one-way

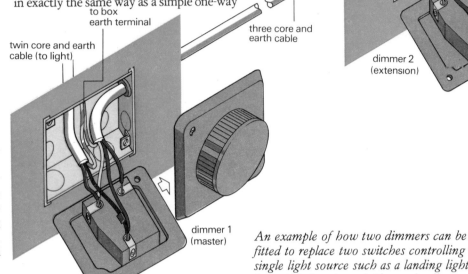

one, but the extra wires involved can cause confusion.

Two-way switch systems are commonly used for lighting the stairs—they're controlled from either the hall or landing. When you dismantle either switch in a two-way system you'll find three core and earth cable instead of the usual two core type. Three core has a red wire, which you can regard as live 'feed' from the mains, and yellow and blue wires which distribute the 'feed' to the light itself between the switch that you are working on and the other two-way switch.

The maker's instructions should be quite specific about which wire goes to which terminal on the new dimmers, so fitting them should present no problems. There is nothing to stop you fitting a dimmer in place of one switch in a two-way system and retaining the existing conventional switch on the other part of the circuit.

If the dimmer is replacing a switch controlling two or more lights on the same circuit, the only restriction is that the dimmer's wattage rating isn't exceeded. Similarly, you can replace a double switch with a single dimmer, although you will of

An example of how two dimmers can be fitted to replace two switches controlling a single light source such as a landing light. It is vital that the red, blue and yellow cores on the three core cable go to the same terminals in both switches—the maker's instructions will specify which they are. The mains feed (red) and switch line (black) cores of the two core light cable connect to the master only. The earths run to the box terminal.

Bear in mind that dimmer switches can be fitted to all types of ordinary lights, but should not be fitted to fluorescent lights. Read the manufacturer's instructions carefully to ensure that the switch you buy matches the output of the light.

course sacrifice individual control: simply make sure that the same wires from each cable are connected to the terminals specified in the instructions.

Problems arise if you try to fit more than two sets of wires to a single dimmer—the terminals simply aren't large enough—and in this case you'd be better to opt for a multigang dimmer retaining individual control. As with all multi-gang switches, the red ('mains live feed') wires from each cable are connected to a common terminal (usually marked C) on the switch backing box. The black switch lines should be connected to separate terminals, one for each control knob.

NEW CEILING LIGHT

The lighting arrangements in many houses amount to just one ceiling rose in the centre of each room with a single pendant lampholder hanging from it by a length of flex. But if you want something better looking or more efficient, you need to know both what's available and just what's involved in making the wiring connections.

Depending on where you go to buy your lighting, you may find a small confusion over the terms used: what you probably know as light bulbs are more correctly called **lamps**; the bits they fit (or screw) into are known as **lampholders** and the whole fitting (excluding the lamp) is known as a **luminaire**. For a normal pendant light the bit hanging on the bottom of the flex is both a lampholder and a luminaire.

Whatever you call them, there's an incredible range of light fittings. A visit to a specialist light shop (or the lighting department of a large department store) or looking through some of the larger lighting catalogues will leave you reeling with the choice. The light fittings that you choose are mainly a matter of taste and design, but the fittings available do divide into a number of types, each of which has its merits and each of which has its own requirements for fitting and wiring up.

Pendant lights: The normal type of pendant light consists of a plastic heat-resisting lampholder suspended from the ceiling rose by a length of two-core flex. (Metal lampholders are not common, but if you have one, bear in mind that any exposed metal parts must be earthed. Alternatively, replace with a plastic type). There's not much you can do with these to make them more interesting apart from choosing interesting lampshades.

Decorative pendant lights: These include lanterns, harp-lamps (styled like old-fashioned oil lamps) and chandeliers. The majority of these will be too heavy to suspend from the flex attached to the ceiling rose and will need some kind of additional or alternative support. With many decorative pendants, the supporting chain and associated hook will be an integral part of the fitting's design. Rise and fall lights should be treated in the same way and fixed to a BESA box mounted in the ceiling.

Spotlights: Spotlights for mounting on ceilings can be single spots or two or three spots mounted on a baseplate or a stalk. Spotlights can produce interesting effects

because the light can be directed. The effect created will depend on the type of lamp (bulb) fitted—an ordinary light bulb (GLS or General Lighting Service lamp), a wide-beam Internally-silvered (IS) lamp or a narrow-beam Crown-silvered (CS) lamp. Spotlights generally have an open baseplate which will mean a special fitting must be used at the ceiling to replace the existing ceiling rose.

Track lights: This system, which is popular in shops, enables a number of spotlights or other lights to be used. The tracks, which are attached to the ceiling, have continuous conductors inside them and the lights are mounted on adaptors which 'plug' in to the track using special clips.

You can position the lights anywhere you like on the track which only needs to be connected to the electricity supply at one end. There are two types of track: single-circuit where all the lights go on and off together, and multi-circuit where you can switch them on and off in two or three

groups. Both types come in a variety of lengths and are available in kits.

If you're replacing a single pendant light with track lighting, be careful not to overload the circuit—lighting circuits are generally designed to cope with up to 12 lamps, assuming that each one is 100W. If the number of lamps you intend using is going to overload the existing circuits, you'll have to run a new circuit from a spare fuseway in the consumer unit. If there is no spare, fit an additional consumer unit.

Track lighting can be fed with flex from

the existing ceiling rose. But if you want to conceal the connections you'll have to remove the existing ceiling rose and, if you've got loop-in wiring, replace it with a junction box.

Fluorescent lights: In terms of light output per unit of electricity, fluorescent lights are by far the most efficient type of light—most other lamps generate more heat than they do light. Fluorescent lights are particularly suitable for kitchens as they throw light over a large area, but the tubes tend to be rather 'cold' in appearance for other rooms.

It's essential that fluorescent lights are **earthed**, which may mean running an earth wire from the consumer unit or electricity board earth—*not* from water or gas pipes—if your lighting circuit doesn't have an earth conductor. Otherwise, the wiring restriction is similar to track lighting (above) except that ordinary dimmer switches can't be used with fluorescent lighting and will have to be replaced by ordinary switches.

Enclosed lights: This type of light is a must in bathrooms, where special safety provisions apply. Most bathroom lights are fairly ordinary globe lights, but there is a range of opal and crystal enclosed lights suitable for living rooms. These will all require the ceiling rose to be removed.

Downlighters: This type of light, which gives a narrow downward beam is mostly used in kitchens, particularly over work surfaces. The downlighter itself is usually in the form of a cylindrical tube which is fully or partially recessed into the ceiling. This means that you cannot use an existing ceiling rose and that you will have to engage in more complicated wiring arrangements as well as cutting holes in the ceiling.

What you need

Apart from normal electrical tools—wire cutter and strippers, pliers, cutting knife and a selection of screwdrivers—you'll need some woodworking tools for cutting and drilling holes in wood and either plasterboard or lath-and-plaster ceilings, depending on what you've got. A stepladder will be handy for obvious reasons.

The electrical accessories you'll need apart from the new light fitting itself will depend on the type of light you are installing. Check through Installing the light, to find out what you need. You'll almost certainly want some plaster or cellulose filler for making good the ceiling if you remove a ceiling rose.

Regulations

In the UK all wiring in houses should be carried out in accordance with the IEE Wiring Regulations. One regulation that is particularly important for replacing ceiling lights is the requirement that the wires and connections to them must be made inside an incombustible enclosure. A ceiling rose meets the requirement, but you're not allowed to have wires waving around in the space above the ceiling since this constitutes a possible fire risk.

Understanding your wiring

Modern lighting circuits are radial—that is the wiring starts at the fuse box (or, more commonly, consumer unit) where it is protected by a 5 amp fuse or circuit breaker and goes from one lighting point to the next until it comes to the last one where it terminates. Normally there will be two lighting circuits in a house—one for the upstairs lights (run in the loft space) and one for the downstairs lights (run between the downstairs ceiling and the upstairs floorboards).

The systems used for the wiring are—**junction box** (also called joint box) and **loop-in**.

In the junction box system, the 'circuit' consists of a cable going from the consumer unit to each box in turn. If this system is fitted, you should be able to spot the boxes.

Each junction box has a supply cable IN and a supply cable OUT—except the last one on the circuit which has only one supply cable going in. There are two other cables connected in to each junction box: one to the light switch and one to the ceiling rose which supplies the light fitting. As

two-core and earth cable is used, the black return wire from the switch is usually sleeved with red PVC insulating tape inside the junction box to show that it is live.

The terminals in the **junction box** are wired as follows:
1. Live supply IN (red).
   Live supply OUT (red).
   Live supply to switch (red).
2. Neutral IN (black).
   Neutral OUT (black).
   Neutral to ceiling rose (black).
3. Live return from switch
   (black & red sleeve).
   Live supply to rose (red).
4. All earth wires (bare & green/yellow sleeve).

The ceiling rose for junction box wiring uses just three terminals—one each for live, neutral and earth. The flex for the light is connected to the appropriate terminals: brown to live, blue to neutral and green/yellow to earth.

In the loop-in system of wiring lights, the ceiling rose also acts as the junction box and all the connections are made there. So there should be three cables in the ceiling rose: one IN, one OUT (except on the last rose in the circuit) and one to the switch. The connections are exactly the same as for the junction box given above except the light flex replaces the cable to the rose.

You can easily tell which system you've got by **turning off the supply** at the mains (it is not enough to turn off the light switch) and then looking inside a ceiling rose and counting the cables coming into it. If there's only one, you've got junction box wiring; if there are three, you've got loop-in wiring. If there are two, it is either the last

The wiring in a junction box rose (below left) is straightforward; a loop-in rose (below) acts as a junction box

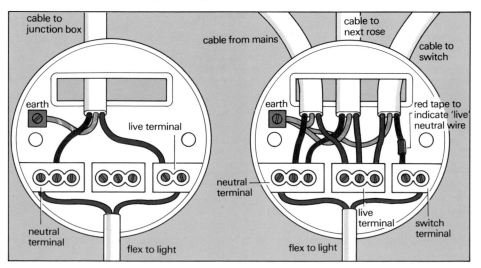

rose on a loop-in system or is a junction box system with an extra light run off the same switch. If it's not obvious, check another rose.

Removing a ceiling rose

You probably won't be able to connect the new light directly to the existing ceiling rose and so you'll have to remove it.

Removing a ceiling rose wired with the **junction box** system is straightforward, since there is only one cable to worry about. Once you've turned off the electricity at the mains and disconnected the existing pendant, the main problem is likely to be in unscrewing the cap of the ceiling rose which may be gummed up with paint. Since you're removing the rose, it won't matter too much if you damage it. Now is the time to check that your wiring is sound. If the cable insulation has started to perish or go brittle, don't go any further but consider having your house rewired—electrical faults are a fire hazard.

If you're using the length of cable that's left poking out of the ceiling—for a fluorescent light or track lighting—there's nothing more to do. But if you're shortening or lengthening the cable to reposition the light fitting, you'll have to continue the work from upstairs—or in the loft, which is much easier.

Shortening isn't much of a problem; lengthening either means putting in an extra junction box (see Fitting a junction box) above the old ceiling rose or running a new length of cable from the junction box for that light.

After you've pulled the cable through the ceiling and done one of these things, make good the hole in the ceiling with plaster or cellulose filler.

> ### ★ WATCH POINT ★
>
> If the hole is very large, push in some screwed-up paper or wire mesh for the plaster to hang on to.

Removing a **loop-in** ceiling rose is a different story: there'll probably be three cables to cope with. To avoid getting them confused when you unscrew the terminals, it's best to twist them together if they come out of the same terminal block. As an extra precaution, work out which cable is which and label them before pulling them up above the ceiling and re-connecting them to a junction box—see Fitting a junction box.

Installing the light

How you fix the light to the ceiling and wire it up will depend on the design. Most lights come complete with a ceiling plate but this may or may not include terminals for the supply connection which must be made in an incombustible enclosure.

A consideration worth bearing in mind before you fix the light is its weight: the maximum weight you can suspend on a 3 amp flex from a standard ceiling rose is 2 kg—anything greater than 2 kg and you must install a special support. But whatever the weight, play safe and attach the fitting to the underside of a joist.

Close-mounted fittings: These are the easiest type to wire up if you have junction box wiring. First screw the support bracket to the joist and then wire up the cable direct to the terminals in the back of the baseplate.

However, if you have loop-in wiring there will be no facility to connect up all the cables and you must fit a junction box to the side of the joist above and lead off a separate cable to the light.

Track lighting: Both track and fluorescent lights must be adequately supported. This inevitably means finding where the joists are.

> ### ★ WATCH POINT ★
>
> The simplest way of locating the joists is by tapping the ceiling with the handle of a screwdriver—a hollow note indicates a void, a solid noise a joist.

You can run the fitting either along or across the joists. If you choose to run it along a joist, you can screw the frame directly into the timber—but make sure that there's enough space to get the cable down through the ceiling.

If you decide to run the fitting across the joists, you will probably find that the screw holes don't coincide with the joists. Get over this problem by screwing an appropriate length of 50mm × 25mm batten to the joists. You can then fix the fitting to the batten.

Track lighting fittings have no facility for wiring loop-in cables so you will have to fit a four-way junction box to an adjacent joist and wire up accordingly—see Fitting a junction box.

Light fittings without terminal blocks: If there are no terminal blocks at the back of the fitting—whichever type you have

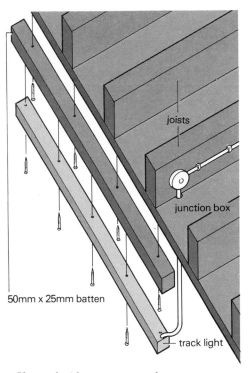

If you decide to run a track system across the joists (above), screw a batten to the underside of the joists first and then fix the track to this

got—you must make the necessary connections to the supply in an 'incombustible enclosure'. The best type is a BESA box (pronounced 'beeza'). This is a plastic terminal conduit box which can be recessed into the ceiling. Choose a BESA box which best suits your location—some have cable outlets in the side, others through the top.

It's best to mount the BESA box to a batten which is fixed between two joists.

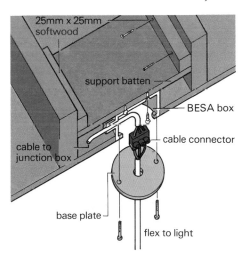

The best way of fixing a recessed BESA box between two joists is to screw it to a support board which bridges the gap. Use two offcuts to join the board to the joists

First locate the joists and then mark the outline of the box on the ceiling between them. Use a padsaw for cutting.

Screw the BESA box to the batten before fixing it in place between the joists. You will need someone else in the room below to make sure that the box is flush with the ceiling.

The electrical connections in the BESA box are made using a 'chocolate bar' cable connector. In theory, both loop-in and junction box connections can be made in the box. However, although you won't have any problem if you have a junction box system, you will probably find that there isn't enough room in the box to make all the connections for a loop-in system. If this is the case, install a junction box nearby and then lead a cable from this to the BESA box where you can connect the cable to the light flex.

Rise and fall lights: More often than not, rise and fall lights are designed to be fitted directly to a BESA box.

Once the BESA box is in place, all you have to do is screw on the bracket, hook on the fitting and wire up the connections.

Chandeliers and heavy pendant lights: These are sometimes sold complete with a hook and bracket but no terminal block. If this is the case, it's best to fit a BESA box for the connections and then fit the bracket and hook to an adjacent joist.

However, there is a device called the Ceiling Master Unit specifically designed to support light fittings (if you have loop-in wiring, you must install a junction box as well).

The Ceiling Master comes in two parts: one incorporates a terminal block for the cable and is screwed to the ceiling; the other slots into it and has a hook for the light fitting together with a second terminal block for the flex. When the two parts are slotted together, electrical contact is made by three spring loaded pins onto three contacts. The Ceiling Master comes in several different finishes.

Fitting a junction box

Junction boxes allow you to tap the power supply from either a loop-in or junction box circuit—safely and securely.

Fitting one is more awkward than difficult and, if there is a room above where you want to install the new light, you will inevitably have to lift floorboards.

Before you start on the job, double check that you have turned off the electricity supply at the mains.

You can fit the junction box directly to a joist—which is more convenient—or to a 75mm × 25mm batten which straddles the void.

How you connect up the cables will depend on the type of lighting circuit you have—junction box or loop-in. The wiring methods are illustrated in the diagrams below. If you want a longer cable in a junction box system, either lead a new cable from the old box or add an extension to the existing cable—making the connections in a three-way junction box.

Points to watch out for are that you use 1mm two core and earth cable; that the bare earth wires are sleeved with yellow/green insulation; and that the neutral return wire from the switch is taped red to show that it is live.

1 *Pencil the outline of the box on the ceiling and cut the shape with a padsaw*

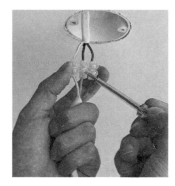

2 *After mounting the BESA box, use a connector strip to join the flex to the cable*

3 *In a Ceiling Master, wire up terminal blocks before slotting the sections together*

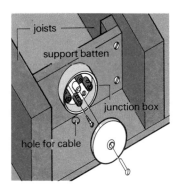

4 *If the hole for the ceiling rose lies between two joists, fit a support board*

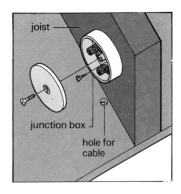

5 *Whenever possible, you will find it best to fix the box to the side of a joist*

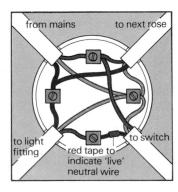

6 *In a loop-in system, install a four-way junction box to replace the old rose*

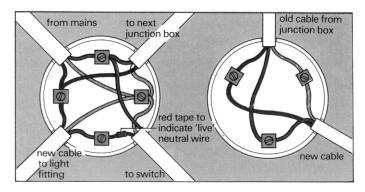

7 *There are two options in a junction box circuit; either run a new cable from the existing junction box (left) or connect an extension to the old cable in a three-way box (right)*

CHAPTER 3

LIGHTING DESIGN

If your existing lighting is inadequate or in the wrong place, now is the time to put things right. There are many alternatives to traditional pendant lights—wall-mounted lights, illuminated ceilings or cupboard lights for instance. And there's no need to stop at the house interior—you can easily extend your lighting out into the garden

FITTING WALL LIGHTS

Lighting is just as much a part of interior decoration as wallpaper, wall colours, furnishings and furniture. Ordinary ceiling mounted lights are a convenient way of illuminating rooms but there's usually less scope for creating interesting light effects. Also, it isn't so easy to tailor the lighting to your individual requirements—for example to provide extra lighting for a dark corner.

The creative use of lighting effects has never been easier to achieve than now, with a myriad of lamps, spotlights and designs on the market. Whilst table lamps and standard lamps are easy to fit, they all have disadvantages: table lamps are often positioned at unsatisfactory eye levels as well as occupying useful table surfaces; standard lamps are awkward and take up valuable floor space. And both types need connection to power sockets which means flex trailing dangerously across the floor.

Wall mounted lights are a much better choice—they're permanent and can be positioned at ideal heights and in places where light is most needed, for instance, to illuminate a picture.

Planning for wall lights

You should always try to avoid any lighting arrangement which causes glare. This is the biggest problem with ceiling mounted lights which need high wattage bulbs to illuminate a room of any size. It's far better to have a number of lower wattage sources providing the same overall level of illumination but without being over-bright at source. Here wall lights ideally fit the bill. For best effect, choose wall lights with their own integral switching so that you can switch in or out any combination of lights. In a room measuring 5m × 4m two wall lights rated at 60 watts will provide adequate light for most purposes.

Where should they go? As a rule of thumb the ideal location is about two-thirds of the way up a wall. In a conventional oblong room, it makes sense to mount two lights on each of the longest walls—about a quarter of the way in from each end. However, not all rooms are symmetrical and if you have any alcoves, beams, nooks

and crannies, try highlighting them for interesting effects.

There are various ways of wiring up wall lights. How complicated you make it depends on the degree of flexibility you want in controlling them. From an operational point of view, the simplest arrangement is to wire the lights so that when you turn on the main light switch the wall lights come on too. And by choosing fittings that have integral switches you'll be able to control the lights individually as well. However, with this simple system you can't have the wall lights on and the main light off. To do this you'll have to install another master switch for the wall lights alone. Although this may sound a more involved job ironically it could make the overall wiring job that much simpler (see page 28). When you come to position this new switch make sure you set it by the entrance door to the room to avoid the dangers of feeling your way across a dark room after the lights have been turned out.

In some situations, and particularly those where you can't get access to the lighting circuits in the ceiling void, it may be easier to take the power for the wall lights from the power circuit via a fused connection unit (see page 28).

Fitting wall lights will mean chasing cables into a wall and pulling up floorboards to pick up the power source. For these reasons it's not a good idea to introduce wall lights soon after new wallpaper has gone up or major painting has been completed. So plan well in advance and remember that in both practical and decorative terms, wall lights are an integral part of interior design.

Bear in mind that the type of wall in the room—timber frame or solid masonry—will affect how the lights will be fitted and the ease with which cables are channelled in. But these will not affect your choice of wall light fitting, the cable you use or the location for the new lights.

What you need for the job

Apart from the light fittings themselves, fortunately you won't need much in the way of materials. Use 1.0mm² PVC sheathed twin core and earth cable for the wiring. How much you need will depend on how you decide to connect the lights, but measure the runs fairly accurately and add

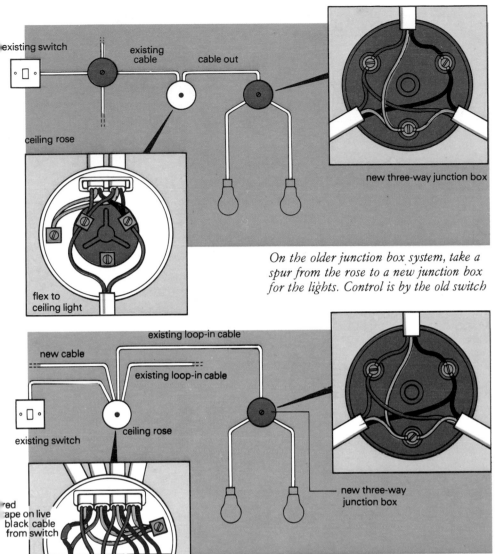

On the older junction box system, take a spur from the rose to a new junction box for the lights. Control is by the old switch

On the modern loop-in system, the connection at the rose is more complicated, but other details are much the same

The cable runs below ceiling level are the simplest of all—the cable should run vertically up the wall from the light and then into the ceiling void. This will ensure that anyone drilling into the wall at a later date will have a good idea of where there is likely to be concealed wiring and so avoid it.

Before channelling the wall use a bradawl to make a small hole at the ceiling/wall junction directly above the light fitting. After breaking through the plaster it should go in easily. If you hit a joist then you can move the run slightly to one side to miss it.

Once you have established the best route, chalk it off on the floor. You have to lift enough floorboards to feed the cable along or through the joists beneath. For the best way to do this see Lifting floorboards. Where cable runs along the joist, it can be fixed to the side of them with cable clips. Where it crosses them, they must be drilled to pass the cable through. Use a 10mm or larger wood bit. Because the joists are close to one another, you won't be able to get the drill in between them. Either drill through at an angle or cut the drill bit off short to fit between the joists. Alternatively, you may be able to get hold of a right angle drilling attachment for an electric drill.

★ WATCH POINT ★

When you drill the holes in the joists, be sure that they are at least 25mm below the top—that way there is no danger of the cables being punctured by nails.

Lifting floorboards

It's easy to make a mess of lifting floorboards unless you know what you're doing. Stick to these rules and you won't have any trouble.
• First remove the skirting boards with a crowbar or stout screwdriver levered on a block of wood.
• If you have a fitted carpet, don't try to pull it up—it will tear or snag on the grippers. The only safe way of releasing the carpet is to force it away from the teeth of the grippers with a bolster or screwdriver underneath.
• Have a look at the boards you want to lift and see if they are complete lengths or if they run underneath a partition wall. In both cases you will have no option but to saw through the floorboards before you can lift them out.

on 10%. You may also need an oval conduit as well as light switches, and three- and four-terminal junction boxes. And don't forget the little things like green/yellow earth sleeving and red insulating tape to mark any switch drops.

It is extremely difficult to channel cable into reinforced concrete or stone walls. If your walls are like this, the best option is to go for surface mounted plastic conduit.

For cable channelling in masonry walls, you need cellulose filler or plaster to patch up the grooves. In plasterboard walls you may additionally need plasterboard for patching.

Depending on the nature of the walls, you will use either masonry plugs, cavity wall fixings and woodscrews to screw the lights to the walls. The size of the screws will vary according to the type of wall lights you are installing and are often supplied.

A good general tool kit should safely see you through the job—the only addition you may have to get are a cold chisel and club hammer if you are channelling into a masonry wall.

Routing the cable

Weigh up the wiring options before deciding which one to go for and always keep the cable runs as simple as possible. Plan carefully how you expect to run the cables from the lights to the power supply—and switch if you choose to have one. Try and anticipate the snags you might come across.

1 *Mark the light position and extend a vertical line*

2 *Chalk out the cable run on the floor above*

3 *Lift floorboards along line of cable. Drill through joists*

4 *To cut a board drill holes so you can insert the blade of a padsaw*

5 *Lever up with a bolster or crowbar against a block*

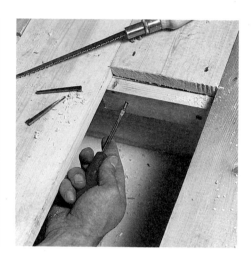

6 *Screw support battens to the sides of the joists*

• If you have to cut the boards, the golden rule is to saw across them near a joist—preferably one near a wall rather than in the middle of the room.

• Locate the joists by sliding a narrow blade between the floorboards. Mark a cutting line across the boards in line with the side of the joist and parallel to the wall.

• If you haven't got a special floorboard saw, drill out a series of 5mm holes along the line so that you can insert a padsaw to cut the boards.

• To free the boards, lever them up on both sides with a bolster. If there are any signs of the boards cracking, ease off—you may be forcing the nails at too tight an angle. Try again on the other side of the offending nails.

• With the boards free from the joists, pull out all the nails with a clawhammer; they can be dangerous—and painful—if trodden on.

• Before replacing the boards, screw 50mm × 25mm support battens to the

joists directly underneath the saw cuts.
• Nail the boards back with flooring brads—they are less likely to split the wood—and then refit the skirting and carpet.

Fixing the cable

Use clips spaced every meter to secure the cable along the joists. Leave plenty of slack where you run it across the joists. Then start channelling the cable where you have marked the position of the wall lights.

There are three options for concealing the cable. Choose whichever is most suitable.

Channelling into a solid wall: Use a cold chisel and club hammer to cut grooves into the wall from the ceiling to where you have marked the position of the wall lights. Cut the channel just deep and wide enough to accept the cable. Take extra care when you cut the channel at the point where the

ceiling joins the wall. Use a small chisel to work from both above and below the ceiling and continue the channel to about 15mm above ceiling level. This will avoid an unsightly bulge in the ceiling where the cable bends into the wall channel. Pull a length of cable down from above and tack it in place in the channel with clips—or better still run it through oval conduit. Plaster over the cable and finish it flush with a straight edge drawn over the wet filler.

Frame wall installation: At the points where you want to fit the lights, drill holes big enough to accept the cables. You may be able to drop the cable through a hole drilled in the top plate into the cavity and pull it out through the holes by hooking it with a piece of still wire. If you encounter an obstruction, it's probably a noggin—a horizontal frame member between the studs. Mark it, then cut out a small section of plasterboard over this point. Cut a notch in the noggin to pass the cable, nail back the plasterboard and patch with filler.

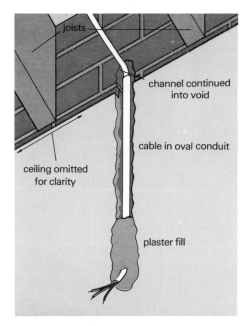

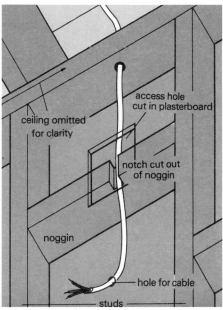

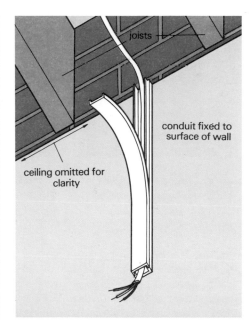

7 *On a masonry wall, channel cable into the plaster. Continue the run above the ceiling*

8 *In a frame wall, pass through the cavity. Cut out to clear any frame cross members*

9 *Alternatively, on any wall, use surface mounted plastic conduit—not so neat, but very easy to fit*

10 *First run the cable above the ceiling. Fix it every metre and leave slack between joists*

11 *Then on a masonry wall, chisel a channel down to the light. Carry it right up into the ceiling void*

12 *Feed the cable into the channel and secure it with clips. Leave plenty spare for connection to the light*

13 *Fill or plaster over the cable and finish off flush with the surrounding wall surface*

Using conduit: Above the light positions drill holes in the ceiling for the cable and screw or glue the backing part of lengths of conduit to the wall—the bottom of the conduit should be just above the place where you want to fit the lights. Feed the cable into the conduit and snap on the cover strips.

★ WATCH POINT ★

It is a good idea to mount the new lights onto wooden backing blocks the same thickness as the conduit. Holes drilled at right angles to each other in the backing blocks will enable the cables to pass straight from the conduit into the wall light.

Wiring up the lights

It makes sense to start off by connecting and fixing the cables to the lights. Only then should you wire up the other ends of the cables into the supply via the junction box. In this way you don't need to turn off the supply until you make the final connections.

Offer the lights up to their marks and use a spirit level to ensure that they are plumb. When you are absolutely sure of their positions, pencil in and then drill the screw holes—it's easier to do this now before the wires are connected.

Cut the cables protruding from the wall back to length which will allow the light fitting to sit snugly against the wall.

Strip back the outer sheathing of the cables by about 50mm and trim off 10mm of insulation from the wires. Slip lengths of green/yellow sleeving over the earth wires and connect up to the appropriate points in the terminal box in the light units—red to L, black to N and green/yellow to E.

With the lights wired up, fix them to the wall using screws and either wallplugs or stud wall fixings.

Before you start connecting to the supply, turn off the electricity at the mains.

If you're installing two wall lights, link their cables together at a three-terminal junction box to simplify the wiring. Set the junction box at a convenient point in the ceiling void or loft space. Connect the red cores of the cables to one terminal block, the black cores to another and the earth cores to a third. From here you can take one cable to connect into the existing lighting circuit.

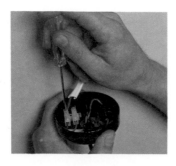

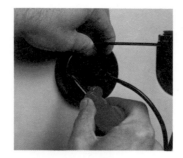

14 *Mark the positions of the fixing holes with the light held in position over the channel*

15 *Strip the cable and screw to the terminals in the light fitting. Remember to sheath the earth wire*

16 *Screw the light into drilled and plugged holes in the wall and check it is secure*

17 *Switch off, then you can connect the new cables into the existing power supply*

Wiring to the existing switch: If you want to use the room's main switch, then you'll have to link the cable from the junction box to the ceiling rose. It doesn't matter if the rose is on a loop-in or junction box system. For ease of working unscrew the rose from the ceiling but keep the cores in their terminals. Feed the new cable through the access hole, taking care not to damage the sheathing.

On a junction box rose take the red core to the live terminal, the black to the neutral and the earth (sleeved in green/yellow PVC) to the earth terminal.

On a loop-in rose first check that there are only one or two power cables going into it together with a switch cable. If there is also a branch supply looped into it then you shouldn't overburden the rose by adding yet another cable. If a connection is feasible then take the red core to the switch terminal and the black to the neutral block. The earth goes to the earth terminal.

Wiring to an independent switch: The best way of wiring is to install a four-terminal junction box at a convenient point on the main feed cable of the lighting circuit. You can then link the wall light cable to this as well as a new cable to a new switch which will give you control of the wall lights independent of the main light (see diagram).

Wiring to a ring circuit: Finally, if you can't take the power from a lighting circuit you can wire the wall lights to a ring circuit. First install a fused connection unit fitted with a 5 amp fuse. Then run 2.5mm² cable to a three-terminal junction box set under the floor. Then take 1.00mm² cable to the wall light.

Before making good the ceiling, walls and floorboards, try the new lights—if they don't work, recheck the wiring.

Finally patch up any holes or damage using plaster or cellulose filler and redecorate around fittings and switches.

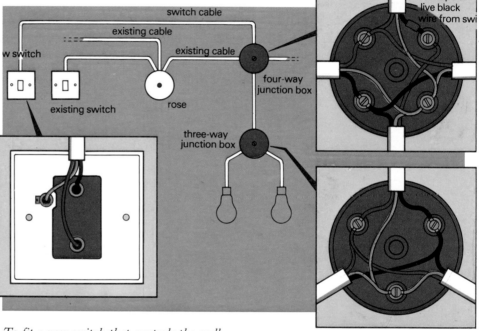

To fit a new switch that controls the wall lights independently of the original switch, cut the existing cable and insert a four-way junction. Connect both the switch cable and the supply for the lights to this. A second junction box divides the supply between the individual wall lights

To power lights from a ring main, break in and insert a junction box. Lead a spur cable up from the junction via a fused spur connector fitted with a 5 amp fuse

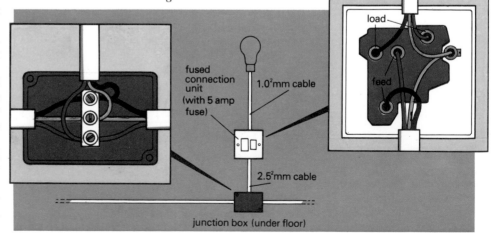

ILLUMINATED CEILING

All too often, ceilings are simply ignored when it comes to planning decor—a great pity, since most of them are a lot less than perfect. Perhaps the ceiling is too high—a common fault in smaller rooms or bathrooms—or is cracked and marked, or maybe it has a rather old fashioned or unsightly heavy cornice.

One of the obvious advantages of an illuminated ceiling is that it enables you to install more diffused, or exciting, lighting—downlighting spotlights, fluorescent tubes (plain or with coloured sleeves) or swivel eye ball lights can all be incorporated. But with different panels and lighting effects to choose from you can, in effect, design your own quite individual ceiling.

If your ceiling is wider than the largest size in the kit range of your choice—it's worth checking because they do vary—you can usually order additional sections of frame to fill out the extra space. In wider rooms, it may also be necessary to give additional support to the structure. The manufacturer's instructions will give guidance as to the spacing of any such supports and indicate the method used. Special brackets normally strengthen extra joins while suspension wires support the span at other points, these being attached to the original ceiling.

Safety is an important consideration, so always choose a kit with panels which have passed the British Standard fire tests (in the UK)—especially if you are putting a ceiling in the kitchen.

Apart from the kit, you need accessories for special lighting effects; most importantly, fluorescent fittings to provide diffused illumination across the entire ceiling. Both these, and direct-light swivel spots which can be recessed into the acoustic type of panel, must be ordered separately. A number of smaller components you'll need for the ceiling assembly must also be specially ordered once you've planned the spaces involved—items like wallplugs, joining brackets, support wires and clips to hold the panels securely in position. You may also need a fine toothed hacksaw to cut the metal supports, plus an electric drill.

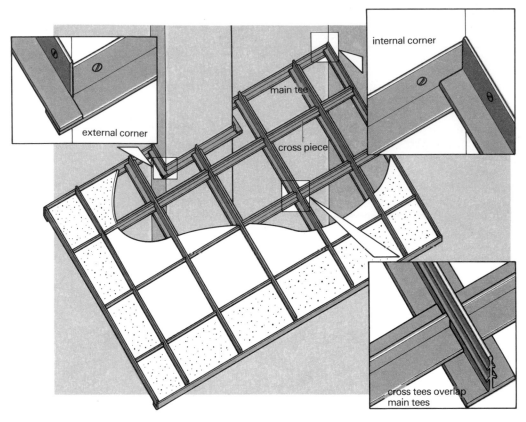

main tee

internal corner

external corner

cross piece

cross tees overlap
main tees

Illuminated ceiling kits consist of a series of translucent or insulating panels laid on an aluminium framework. The main tees are supported by a side framework screwed to the walls; the cross pieces rest on the main tees. There is normally no need to secure the panels—they simply rest in place on top of the aluminium framework. To avoid high spots of light, the fluorescent tubes should be positioned so they run directly above the main tees

Planning considerations

The first thing to consider is the height of your new ceiling. Building regulations in the UK require a minimum of 2.3m from the floor over at least half the area in a habitable room. Because of the fixing and lighting requirements, the illuminated ceiling must be at least 100mm below the level of the existing one (50mm will suffice if you use the acoustic panels without lighting).

Bear in mind that the height of the top of the existing window recesses may affect your intended ceiling height—you must install the ceiling *above* window recesses to avoid unnecessary work, or blocking the light and even creating changes in level.

Measure the ceiling, make an accurate scale plan, then divide it into squares to represent the panels. Some firms supply a ready-squared diagram as part of their order form so that you can transfer your ceiling measurements on to it. Always check your measurements twice.

If your ceiling will not take an exact number of whole panels—and the chances are that it won't—calculating the number of panels you need is slightly more tricky. You don't want to have part panels at one side of your ceiling only—they should be evenly spaced at both borders for a balanced look. So find the centre of the room by measuring across between walls. Take recesses into account—the centre of the new ceiling should be centred on the widest part of the room.

You don't normally need to provide details about the framework when you order. Give the firm the ceiling size and they will send you appropriate framework.

Next decide on the colour, pattern and texture of panels you want. Here, bear in mind the existing decor and colours in your room and the finish of the framework you've chosen. You don't have to use the same type of panel across the entire grid. The whole ceiling can be covered with translucents, you can have a patchwork effect by mixing them with acoustics, or you might want illumination in the central portion and opaques round the borders. And you can mix and match any number of different colours, too.

Supports: How many and what type you'll need depends on the kind of kit you have opted for—so check the manufacturer's brochure for distances between supports (it could be anything from 1,220mm to 3m).

If a system of brackets is used at joins in the main framework, calculate how many you'll need by looking at your measurements and the maximum length in which the components are supplied. Wire supports are available in packets of ten, each one 1m long. Here again, work out how many you need by taking the length of your main runners and checking how many supports are recommended for that length. Then you must multiply by the number of main tees you have in your framework.

Screw eyes to secure the suspension wires to the ceiling must also be ordered—sufficient to cope with the wires and perhaps a couple of extra ones.

Lighting: Allow about 1.5 watts per square foot of ceiling when working out how many lights you'll need.

Decide now whether you want to have all fluorescents or a mixture of these and downlights round the edges, for example. If you pick fluorescents make sure you get the correct type of fitting for your ceiling level—batten units with a full-length bracket-type fixing are best for a drop of 150mm or more, compact units which have the tubes fixed directly to the ceiling with clips are useful for lesser drops.

Ventilation: To avoid condensation problems later insert a plastic ventilation grille into a panel at either end of the ceiling.

Preparing the ceiling

Before you begin to prepare the existing ceiling, clear the room as much as you can. Take out any furniture which can be moved, cover the rest and either take up floorcoverings or cover them with a large sheet of polythene or a dust sheet.

First, find the joists and mark them so that if you want these for fixing support wires or lights later, you won't have to waste time trying to locate them. Take a screwdriver and tap the ceiling with the handle. When you hear a dull thud instead of a hollow sound, you know you've hit the joist. Mark it in pencil and then proceed to locate the others. You'll find in most cases that joists are 400mm to 450mm apart.

Next, check on the condition of your ceiling and decide whether some renovation work is required at this point. Fill any cracks with fine surface interior filler and

★ WATCH POINT ★

There are exceptions to everything
—so always check the spacing!
Gently push a bradawl into the
ceiling where you reckon the joist
should be, twisting it from side to side
as you go.

sand smooth. If the paint or whitewash
appears to be flaking off in parts, rub it down
and give the whole area a coat of stabilising
solution.

When this had dried—or if your ceiling
hasn't required an application of stabilising
solution—give it a coat of brilliant white
emulsion paint (two coats are even better).
The white paint helps to reflect a maximum
amount of light through the panels of the
new false ceiling.

★ WATCH POINT ★

A coat of white paint may obscure the
pencil marks locating the joists. So to
make sure they are still visible when
you need them, tap a pin securely
into the surface of the ceiling where
the marks are. You can paint round
the pin without dislodging it.

The next marking up job is for the side
framework to be fixed round the walls. You
should have already decided at what height
to install your illuminated ceiling. Don't
consider changing the level at this point
because you will already have ordered the
appropriate light fittings for the level you
originally chose.

Mark where the line is to go, after
measuring carefully. Continue the line right
round all four walls of the room. It's
extremely important to get it absolutely
horizontal, so don't rush this marking
job—use a spirit level as you go along and
use a straight edge (like a timber batten) to
rule the line. Use as long a spirit level as you
can. If you haven't got a builder's level, or
cannot hire one, simply tie a long batten to a
small level and use that. Using a small level
on its own invites awkward discrepancies.

Light fixings

Before you start putting up the ceiling
framework, the lights must be positioned
and then wired up. Mark the positions
where these are to go. If they are not near

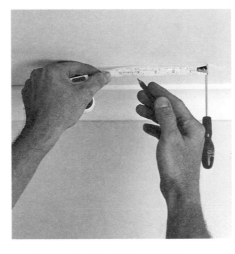

1 *Locate the first joist, mark its
position with a bradawl and measure
to next joist*

2 *Establish the lowest point of the
ceiling then mark round the walls for
the side frame*

3 *Snap chalk lines to show where the
tees fit. Light fittings should always
align with them*

joists, drill the ceiling plaster carefully
where you have marked it, insert a toggle
type cavity plug and screw the fittings into
the ceiling. The clips which hold the
compact type units will require similar
plugs so that you can screw their clips in
place.

If the gap between the old ceiling and the
new is less than 100mm, position the lights
where the struts of the frame will go to
avoid any risk of overheating and damage to
panels. You can check the relevant strut
positions by referring back to your original
scale plan of the ceiling.

The next step is the wiring and since the
light units are all pre-wired this should be
fairly straightforward. First switch off the
electricity at the mains. Some pre-planning
is useful here so that the supply is disconnected for the minimum length of time.

Undo the cover of the ceiling rose and
take a look at what sort it is. If it is an old-
fashioned two terminal rose, remove it and
replace it with a three terminal junction
box. You simply undo the wood screws
which hold the rose to the ceiling and take
out the mains wires from the terminals.
Take care that you don't push the cable out
of reach into the ceiling cavity. There will
be some slack in the mains cable so ease it
out of the ceiling cavity.

Secure a three terminal junction box
where the rose was located, fastening the
mains wires, one to each of the terminal
blocks (if there is no earthing wire, you
must run one from the main consumer unit
to the junction boxes).

Modern type rose: If you have a modern
loop-in kind of ceiling rose (this will have a
terminal block with three separate sections
set into it and an earth connector), you can
leave it in place. Replace the pendant flex
with a length of new 1mm² twin and earth
cable and run this to a new junction box as
before. Make sure that the new box is firmly
secured to the ceiling.

In the case of either kind of rose, the new
cables run to the ballast starter units for
each fluorescent—fly leads connect the
starter ballasts to the individual tubes.
Secure the new cable to the ceiling with
cable clips at 300mm intervals.

Using this method the lights will be
controlled from the existing switching
arrangement.

Though the wires of the switch are
colour-coded (red for live, black for neutral)
they are both effectively 'live'. For future
reference and safety, stick red tape round
the ends of the black wire to indicate that it
is a 'switched live' wire.

Independent control of the lighting

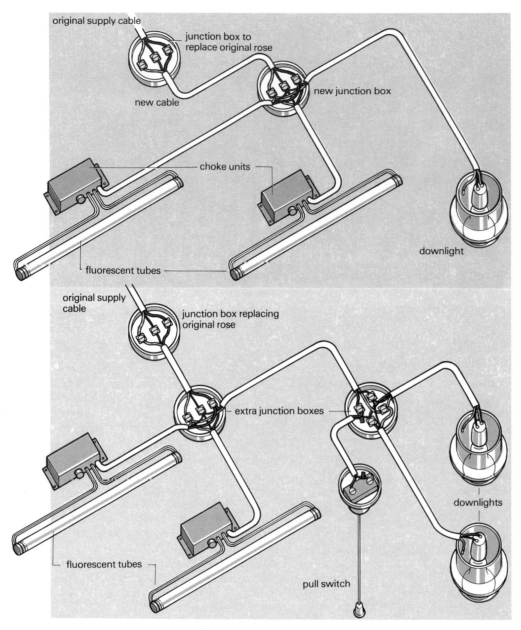

original supply cable

junction box to replace original rose

new cable

new junction box

choke units

downlight

fluorescent tubes

original supply cable

junction box replacing original rose

extra junction boxes

downlights

fluorescent tubes

pull switch

4 *Switch off the electricity, unscrew the rose cover and remove the pendant flex*

5 *Secure the heavy ballast units to a joist or a batten run between two joists*

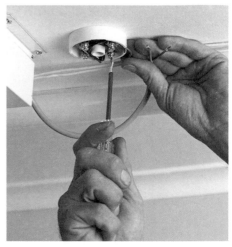

6 *Run the cable from the ballast unit to a new junction box and make the connections*

Top: The simplest wiring arrangement. Take a feed for each light from a new junction box. The lights are then controlled by the original switch

Above: To give independent control of downlights, you can incorporate a pull switch in our wiring arrangement. You will need to buy an additional junction box for this, however

circuits can be achieved by duplicating and extending the above wiring circuit with additional four-terminal junction boxes. A cable is taken from the three-terminal junction box to each of any number of four terminal junction boxes (see diagram above). A pull-cord switch is wired into each four-terminal box in the manner

described above. Finally the units to be controlled by each pull switch are wired into the junction box.

Wiring for the downlighters should be done at the same as that for fluorescents although the lights will not be connected until the ceiling panels are added.

Installing the framework

Start with the right angled edge trim round the walls. Measure the distance along the line you have already marked out, from corner to corner on the first wall—measure twice to be sure you get it right.

Having established the length of metal angle you'll need, cut it with a hacksaw, filing off any rough edges. Sections which

7 *Go round the wall marking the fixing positions for the side framework. Make sure they are absolutely level*

8 *Position the main tees. For accuracy use the cross tees or panels as a spacing guide*

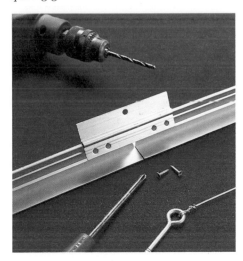

9 *You may need to extend the main tees. If so, use the brackets supplied by the manufacturer*

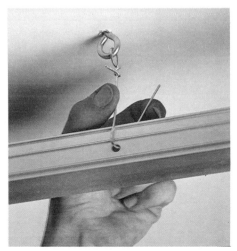

10 *Add suspension wire supports as required. Fix the screw eye into the nearest joist*

butt together should be cut straight using a try square as a guide.

When you have cut the first piece, drill holes in it at 550mm intervals, file off any burrs then place the section against the wall along the line. Mark the hole positions, remove the frame and drill for fixing with suitable wallplugs. For solid walls any kind of plastic or wallplug will do; for stud partition walls get the cavity fixing with a butterfly flange. As you put up each section, do a quick check with a spirit level to make sure the alignment is correct.

> ### ★ WATCH POINT ★
>
> If the wall isn't absolutely flat, the frame may have to be adjusted. To do this, release or tighten the screws until it lies as straight as possible. Any gaps can be packed temporarily with small pieces of wood and filled properly.

Main tees: With the edge support installed, add the main tees. To avoid joins, place these across the shortest span of the room.

Start by marking their positions on the edge framing. Unless the ceiling is a regular shape that matches a whole number of 600mm square panels then you will have to cut panels at the borders, so you must take account of this in marking for the tees.

Measure between opposite walls, find the centre point and work from that. Use either a cross tee or a panel to check the spacings between components as you go.

When the points are marked, measure between corresponding marks on opposite walls so that you can cut and install the first tee. Before you do any cutting, check the manufacturer's instructions to make sure that there are no special indents or slotting-in points in the main tees to accept the shorter cross tees.

If the manufacturer recommends suspension wire supports over specific distances (this varies according to the type of framework), add these as you go along. Drill a hole in the tee at the recommended distance, loop the wire through and attach it to a screw eye fixed into a ceiling joist at the nearest appropriate point.

> ### ★ WATCH POINT ★
>
> Measure the distance between opposite points on the wall for **every** tee. Don't assume the distances will be the same for all because there may be variations if the walls are not precisely parallel.

Joining framework

Joins on the main tees must be supported by brackets. These will not be so obvious when the ceiling is completed, but joins on the edge trim—either in a straight run or at corners—will be visible from below, so it's worth taking the time and trouble to achieve a really neat join. There are different ways of cutting for different joins.
For a straight length: To join two straight lengths you need a butt joint. Make sure that the angle on both pieces is 90°. Use a square as a guide and mark your cutting line, preferably with a metal scribe or with a very sharp pencil.

Support the section to be cut on a stable surface. It's best if you can sit it firmly against a wooden stop or bench hook to prevent the angle moving.

Cut along the line with a fine toothed hacksaw—through both faces at once. Then take a fine flat file and remove rough edges and burrs.
At a corner: You have a choice of two cutting and joining methods here. Use an overlap join for an internal corner—it's made in the same way as a butt joint, except that you measure up to remove extra material to make the overlap.

Adding the panels

Once the main tees are in position, the cross tees and panels can be slotted into place.

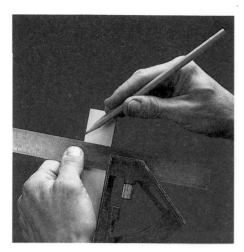

To get a true 90° cut for a butt joint use a square and with a metal scribe mark your cutting line

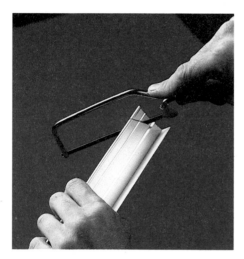

Cut across with a fine toothed hacksaw. Then cut the rib back slightly so it fits easily

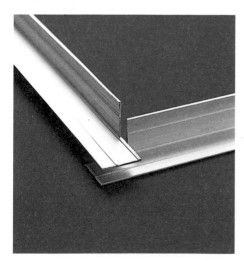

External joints should overlap. They require careful marking and cutting for neat results

Remember that you will, no doubt, have part panels at the border so start with the cross tees and panels at the centre of the room and work outward. First find the centre point.

Mark the position of your cross tees from the centre point and then slot in a cross tee and its panel—the panel generally sits on top of the tees. Check instructions on the exact way to fit the cross tees—some slot into the main tees, others just sit neatly on top of them.

You can, of course, fit all the cross tees first and then slot in the panels, but since you will almost certainly have to move the tee to position the panel it's usually easier to put in one cross tee, one panel, slide the next cross tee into place, put in another panel and so on.

Although not essential, panel clips will hold the panels securely in place, so if you've ordered them with your kit, use them as you proceed from panel to panel.

Border panels: Cut these to size after the central section is complete. Measure the gap between the centre of the last tee and the edge trim on the wall.

Don't, whatever you do, cut them too small or they may simply fall through the framework. Transfer these measurements onto the panels using a felt-tipped pen. Measure twice, cut once. Don't assume every panel to be the same measurement; do each one individually.

Ventilation: It's worth providing ventilation with two plastic grilles. Install them in complete tiles once the panels are in place and you're sure that they all fit.

Downlights: To fit these in acoustic panels, take out the appropriate panels and cut a hole in the centre of each fractionally smaller than the light's external diameter.

Cut the hole with a padsaw, smooth the edges and then put it back in position on the ceiling grid. Cut two wooden battens to fit across the top of the main runner on each side of the hole, then gently push the lamp through the hole you've cut and adjust its fixing prong so that they sit securely on the battens. Assemble the rest of the light and it can then be wired to the connections which you have already prepared.

★ WATCH POINT ★

Try to keep the panels clean—PVC ones in particular mark easily. Wear a pair of cotton gloves or use pads of cloth to hold the edges as you slot in the panels.

11 Lay the panels in position adjusting the cross tees for each one as you work if necessary

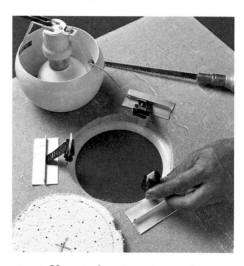

12 Use a padsaw to cut acoustic panels ready for downlights or ventilation grilles

13 If you need to cut translucent panels, cut oversize and fold up edge as a supporting rib

AUTOMATIC CUPBOARD LIGHT

A small striplight in a display cabinet instantly enhances ornaments and glassware and similar lights in deep, dark kitchen cabinets are an invaluable practical aid.

In many instances it's sufficient just to be able to turn on the light when it's required, but there are situations where it is extremely useful to have a light that comes on automatically, for example, when a cupboard door is opened. The facility has been standard on refrigerators for a good number of years and is now a common feature on drinks cabinets.

Automatic lighting is made possible by a device known as a push-to-break switch. This consists of a spring-loaded plunger which is held depressed by a cupboard door when closed. In this position it 'breaks' the circuit to the light which therefore goes off. But when the door is opened, the plunger springs out and the circuit is connected.

Automatic lights have a number of applications. Kitchen units, for example, are an obvious choice—particularly the floor cupboards where you have to bend right down to see into the back of them. But understairs cupboards, bathroom cabinets, walk in wardrobes and writing bureaux can all benefit too.

Choosing a light fixture

Automatic switches can be used to control most types of light fitting, but for many of the locations where you'll be fitting cupboard lights, small striplights or fluorescent tubes are the obvious choice.

Striplights tend to be more popular, but this is probably due to the fact that they are much cheaper to buy than a fluorescent unit. However, there are a number of advantages in using a fluorescent tube, once the initial cost has been absorbed. For example, you only need a tube rated at a quarter of the wattage of a striplight to give out roughly the same amount of light, and the tube will last up to five times longer, so they are more economical to run. Unlike a striplight a fluorescent tube doesn't heat up which is a point well worth bearing in mind if you're not too sure about the quality of the veneer or melamine finish of the cupboard you're fitting the light to. The heat

from striplights can lift veneers and discolour melamine.

Fluorescent tubes are also sometimes fitted with diffusers to help give an even spread of light, and added protection against the effects of steam.

When you buy the fitting, check the maximum size of the lamp it will take. Remember, you are lighting a confined space, so in most cases you're only going to need low wattage lights. Small cupboards may only need a 15W striplight, with larger ones needing 25W or 30W lamps. Sometimes in very large cabinets you may even need to wire two 30W fittings together to give a good spread of light. What you must never do, however tempting, is to exceed the maximum wattage of the fitting when you want to produce more light.

The simplest way of providing an automatic light, both from the installation and wiring point of view, is to use a fitting which combines the lamp and switch in one unit. Naturally, these units are more bulky, and therefore slightly more conspicuous than a separate switch and light, but this is a minor disadvantage. The units incorporate a heat deflector and a reflector under the bulb so that the maximum amount of light is thrown into the cupboard, and there is no damage from heat to the cupboard's surface.

If you are mounting a light in the larder or understairs cupboard, you need something more than a small striplight or fluorescent tube to illuminate it. In this instance, there's nothing to stop you connecting an automatic switch to an ordinary battenholder to which you can fit a 100W light bulb. The battenholder could

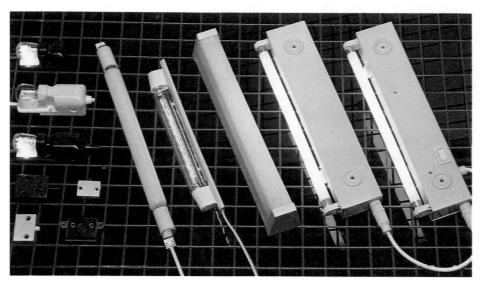

A variety of fittings can be used for cupboard lighting. 'Pigmy' lights (on the left) may be fitted with their own switch. Otherwise you need a separate switch (bottom left). These will also control strip and fluorescent lights (centre and right)

be set on the ceiling, although there is a type with an angled socket which enables you to mount the light on the wall. Try to pick a spot in the cupboard that will minimize the amount of shadow cast by any shelves. Again, the wider spread of light from a fluorescent light fitted with a diffuser will help alleviate this problem.

If required, you can operate more than one light from the same automatic switch. So if you have a cupboard with three solid shelves and you want to illuminate each one, you can loop together three 15W or 30W fittings and then connect these to the switch. The actual wiring involved will depend on the method you use to obtain the electricity supply. However, if you want to connect fluorescent lights, it's not just a simple matter of looping together the terminals in each fitting. By far the easiest method is to buy fittings that can be joined using special connectors.

The main factor governing the number of lights that can be controlled from one switch is the amp rating of the switch itself. Usually this is 1 amp. Because domestic electricity in the UK is supplied at around 240 volts this means that such a switch can control up to 240W of light or eight 30W striplights, for example. But the situations where you'll need this capacity are extremely rare.

However, there is one other thing to remember if you are taking the power from a lighting circuit. A modern domestic lighting circuit has the capacity to supply power to light fittings which in total don't exceed 1200W (light bulbs under 100W counting as 100W). So calculate the wattage of the lights on the circuit you intend adding to just to make sure you're not going over the limit. But unless you've already made considerable additions to the circuit it's doubtful that you'll exceed the maximum load.

Tools and materials

Aside from the light fixture and switch there is very little else that you will need for this job. If you are going to take your power from an existing socket you will need a 3 amp plug and a length of flex. When calculating the amount of flex that you will require, measure fairly accurately and add a 10 per cent allowance to arrive at the total amount of flex to buy. If you want to change the colour of the flex at some point along the run, you will also need a flex connector to join one length to another.

If you are going to break into a circuit to obtain your power supply, then you will need a four terminal junction box. In a bathroom you will need to use an unswitched fused connection unit to take a spur from a nearby outlet.

In the way of tools, you'll need a cold chisel and club hammer to cut a channel in a masonry wall as well as conduit and cable clips. The screws you require will most likely be included with the fixture and switch. Don't forget a bit of red PVC tape to mark a live neutral returning to a junction box from a switch, and a little filler to make good any channels you have cut. Also have to hand a small screwdriver, drill, wire cutters, a sharp knife, and a filling knife to finish off.

Installing the switch and fixture

Usually there is little more to mounting a switch and light fixture than screwing them into place through the insulated screw holes moulded into the casing. But for them to work effectively, it's the positioning that's all important.

It's usually not critical how you site the switch and light in relation to one another —although the closer they are, the neater you can make the wiring runs. And if you can take the wiring in a corner or under a shelf, so much the better. See Wiring up the circuit, for what's involved.

Fitting the switch

Site the switch on the cabinet or door frame so that the top leading edge of the door or flap closes against the plunger. This means the light will come on almost immediately and turn off later than if the switch was mounted on the hinge side of the cupboard.

In the case of a door frame, you'll probably have to cut a notch in the door stop to conceal and protect the switch as much as possible. Hiding switches in cabinets is a little more difficult, but if you use one with a white casing on white or light-coloured furniture and one with a brown casing on a natural wood finish, they shouldn't be too conspicuous once they are installed.

Depending on the design of the cabinet, however, you may be able to mortise the switch into the frame, concealing the mechanism almost entirely. The plunger may protrude through a metal plate (which should be earthed) which holds the switch in place. If you are building your own cabinet you may also be able to incorporate the switch into the design, so that a baffle at the front concealing the light fitting can also house the switch.

Fitting the light

If you are making or assembling a cabinet, it's relatively easy to incorporate the light into the design. One favourite place is a cutaway at the back of a shelf so that light can be thrown up and down the back panel. It's an economical arrangement as well because one fitting can effectively light two bays of the cabinet.

But if you're fitting lights into a cabinet

1 *Position the switch where it will be operated by the door's outer edge, and mark around the case*

2 *You may need to saw or chisel out a housing to allow the switch to fit neatly and to protect it from knocks*

3 *Position the light in a convenient spot and mark fixing holes through the case using a bradawl*

that initially wasn't designed for them, siting the lights here isn't really a practical option unless you are prepared to alter the structure. Instead you'll have to look for an alternative location. Remember, it's the effect of the lights you'll want to see and not necessarily the fittings themselves. Wherever possible try to hide the lights unless you are using a light which is attractive to look at. You can, for example, buy a striplight with an opal tube that obscures the tungsten element and in so doing gives a less glaring light. This is particularly valuable where you only want illumination for aesthetic purposes.

The easiest method of concealment is to fit a baffle under the top front edge of the cabinet and screw the fitting to this. If you can match the finish of the baffle to the rest of the cupboard it will look as though it's part of the original design. The baffle will also help direct light into the cupboard. And for greater effect in a drinks cabinet cover the base with a mirror so that light is also reflected back under the glasses. Baffles are particularly important in kitchen units because they protect the light from being knocked accidentally as you put away cans and saucepans and other awkward objects.

Making a baffle

If the cabinet you want to light has adjustable shelves then it is quite simple to create an arrangement where you can light two bays with one light fitting. You can cut the baffle from one of the shelves. Remove the upper shelf to the two bays you want to light and mark a line along the length approximately 65mm from the back edge. Carefully cut along this line using a panel saw. Use this offcut as the baffle. You will have to finish the rough edge of the baffle to match the rest of the surrounding surface. The easiest method is to use iron-on tape.

Mark the baffle so that it is centred along the edge of the shelf and so it projects the same distance above and below the shelf. Drill countersink holes at approximately 200mm centres along the length of the baffle. Drill pilot holes and screw the baffle to the shelf. You may find that the shelf no longer fits on its supports properly therefore you may also have to readjust the position of the shelf supports. Once you have the shelf-baffle combination completed, you're ready to wire up the light fitting and switch in the ordinary way. However, you will find it easier to fix the light fitting to the baffle if you remove the shelf/baffle from the cabinet. Also if you have to drill through

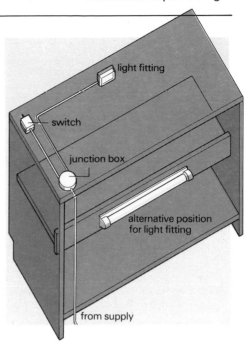

There are several alternative positions for the light and switch. Decide the best and then work out neat routes for the wiring using a junction box as necessary.

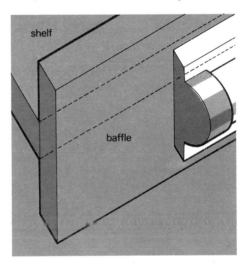

You can fit a striplight to the back of a shelf if you cut away a section and then add a baffle to protect the fitting

the back wall of the cabinet for the flex entry, you should drill the hole opposite the baffle so that it is hidden.

Wiring up the circuit

Once the switch and light fitting are positioned, you've got the task of connecting them to a suitable power source.

Basically, you've got three options on how you provide a supply of electricity.
Plugging into a socket outlet: By far the easiest and simplest method of providing

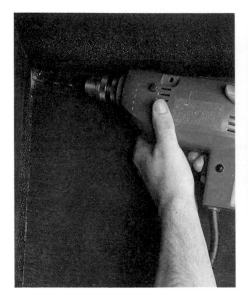

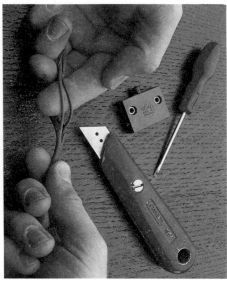

a small hole through the back panel where the side and top panels meet. Thread the flex through the hole and neatly run it along this join until you reach the switch position. Here you have to make what's known as a 'window' in the flex. This entails removing a section of sheathing very carefully without damaging the insulation on the cores underneath.

To make the window, use a sharp cutting knife to slice down the length of the flex and then to circle round it at each end. How much sheathing you have to remove depends on the size of the switch. Don't overcut, as you can always remove a little more sheathing as required—you can't add it. Next, test that you haven't nicked the insulation on the cores by doubling the flex over to see if there are any splits revealing bare metal.

Now you can make the connection to the switch itself. Cut the 'live' (brown) core and strip back about 6mm of insulation from the ends. Secure these ends in the terminals either side of the plunger/switch mechanism. The neutral (blue) core doesn't have to be cut, it is just looped round (see diagram below).

Draw the sections of flex each side of the 'window' together and set them under the cord clamp so that the flex can't be pulled from the body of the switch. Run the flex

4 *Drill a hole in a concealed corner at the back of the cabinet in order to admit the flex which connects to the power supply*

5 *Strip away the sheathing from the flex to form a 'window' for the switch. Take great care not to cut the inner insulation*

power is to plug into a three-pin 13 amp socket outlet. It's a means most commonly used for wall units, cupboards, cabinets and wardrobes in the living room, dining room or bedroom.

Usually there's a free socket near floor-level which is close enough to provide a supply. And because the plug can be easily pulled out you've got no problems of disconnection should you want to change the units around. You simply find another convenient socket to plug in to.

The three-pin plug must be fitted with a 3 amp fuse and wired with 0.5mm² flex. Whether you use two-core or three-core flex depends on the type of switch and fitting being installed. If they are double insulated, they don't need to be earthed, so two-core

flex can be used. But if the light fitting, for example, has an exposed metal base, and the switch is held into a mortise with a metal plate, these will need to be earthed so use three-core flex. This is not very common on most new light fittings and switches because they are held in place with plastic casings which eliminates the problem.

From the plug, run white-sheathed flex clipped along the top of the skirting to the back of the unit or cabinet. Here you may want to fit a flex connector so you can change the colour of the sheathing. A brown-sheathed flex, for instance, will look less conspicuous against a natural wood surface than white flex, which is better used on white melamine.

Run a flex up the back of the unit and drill

★ **WATCH POINT** ★

You will be dealing with small terminals and pieces of equipment set in awkward corners so you may find it easier to remove the switch and light temporarily while you make the wiring connections.

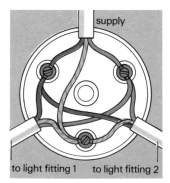

Use a three terminal junction box to wire up more than one light fitting controlled from the same switch. Connect all the like cores

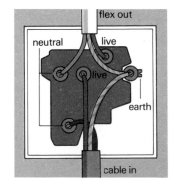

To take your power supply from a fused connection unit connect the supply cable to the feed side, and the flex to the load side

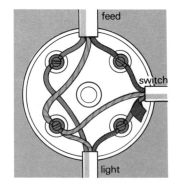

Use a four terminal junction box if you are running a separate flex to the switch and light fitting. Flag live/neutral with red PVC tape

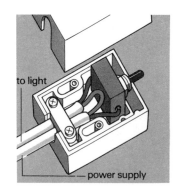

Most new switches do not need earthing as they have plastic casings. Cut a window in the flex and connect split live cores to the switch

onto the light fitting, strip back the sheathing and insulation from the cores and connect them to the relevant terminals.

If earthing is required either at the switch or light, run the circuit in three-core flex. At the switch you may have to improvise a little if there is no earthing terminal to connect the mortise fixing plate to the earth continuity. You could wrap the earth core round one of the fixing screws but make sure you don't break the continuity to the light. If this needs to be earthed, there's usually a terminal for it near the live and neutral terminals.

Only after all the wiring is complete and all the protective covers set in place should you plug in to test the light.

Connecting to a lighting circuit: This is an ideal method of providing power if you are installing an automatic light in kitchen wall units, a bathroom cabinet or an understairs cupboard. In a kitchen, for example, you'll probably want every socket outlet there is for running electrical appliances, so taking one over permanently for automatic cupboard lights isn't satisfactory. If you've got a spare socket at floor level, you've still got the problem of concealing the flex as it runs up into the cupboards, whereas by taking the power from the lighting circuit above, the cable can drop down neatly into the top of the units unseen.

For ease of wiring, use the junction box system. Decide on where to site the switch and light, then run 1.0mm² two-core and earth cable back from these to a four-terminal junction box fixed in the top corner in the picture. Ignore the earth core if it isn't needed and cut or tape it back; if it is make sure it is sheathed in green/yellow sleeving. And remember that both the cores in the cable leading to the switch are 'live' so the black core should be flagged in red PVC insulating tape to indicate this. Connect one core to the terminal on one side of the plunger and the other to the terminal opposite.

From the four-terminal junction box run a 1.0mm² cable back to the lighting circuit and connect it into the main supply with a three-terminal junction box. Make sure that power to the circuit has been turned off before you do this.

If you're installing the light in a larder, however, you may find it easier to insert a four-terminal junction box directly into the main lighting circuit and then run a cable to the light and another to the switch.

In a small bathroom cabinet you may be able to get away with a third variation in this system of wiring. In fact it's virtually the same as the wiring from a socket outlet.

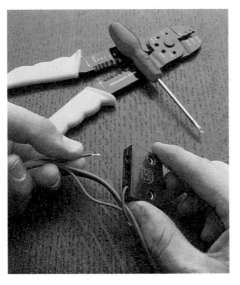

6 *Cut the brown 'live' core and strip the ends so you can connect them into the two terminals of the switch*

7 *Strip the ends of the flex back so that you can connect them into the terminals in the light fitting*

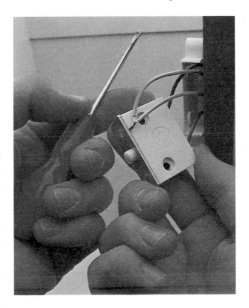

8 *On metal-cased switches where there is no earth terminal, connect an earth wire to one of the case fixing screws*

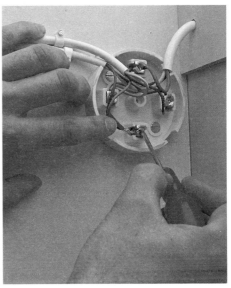

9 *If you fit two lights, use a junction box to split the supply to each of the fittings and the light switch*

You have to cut a 'window' in the 1.0mm² cable to fit the switch and then the cable is taken on to connect to the light. The cable should then be joined to the lighting circuit in a three-terminal junction box.

Power via a fused connection unit: You may be faced with the situation where there are no convenient socket outlets (as in the case of a bathroom) and where access to the lighting in the ceiling void is not very easy. If you're installing the automatic light in, say, the living room then the obvious thing to do is to fit a new double socket at the end of a spur from the ring circuit. But you

can't do this in the bathroom. Here the answer is to fit an unswitched fused connection unit at the end of a spur from the ring circuit and then to run a 0.5mm² flex from the load side of the unit to the push-to-break switch and then onto the light as if you were wiring the system from a socket outlet. The connection unit should be fitted with a 3 amp fuse. Ideally it should be sited as near to the cabinet as possible which, unfortunately, may mean cutting a long chase for the spur cable if you are flush mounting the wiring. Any surface wiring should be run in wall-mounted, plastic trunking.

GARDEN LIGHTING

There are many different types of outdoor lights, and they can be classified in a number of different ways. Perhaps the most useful way of looking at them is by how and where they can be fixed, since this determines to a large extent how easy or difficult they will be to install.

Wall-mounted lights: The main virtue of lights fixed to a house wall is that they will be easy and cheap to wire up. Several different patterns are available.

The simplest are porch lights—in the shape of old-fashioned carriage lanterns, modern globe lights, 'brick' lights, or the more utilitarian bulkhead lights. All these use normal GLS (general lighting service) bulbs like the ones used in most indoor light fittings. In a clear glass fitting, a 60W bulb will appear very bright in the dark, and may dazzle; though the light will be softer and easier on the eye if the light has a translucent, diffusing, cover. If you use a porch light on an outside wall, make very certain it is designed for outdoor use; lights marked as *jet-proof* will be, but others should be carefully checked.

Spotlights can be mounted on house walls, too, but it is vital that you get a type which is designed for outdoor use—this will use a PAR (parabolic aluminized reflector) bulb which has a specially-strengthened glass front. It is easy to dazzle people with spotlights, so they are best mounted high up, where they can cover a whole area with light. Note that PAR38 bulbs should be available in both spot and flood versions— the spot type covers a smaller area, but gives a more intense light; the flood version will light a larger area but to a lower lighting level overall.

For the brightest light over a large area, a special tungsten halogen floodlight can be used. These are usually mounted high on a building, or on top of a pole, but some types are designed for use at ground level, primarily for floodlighting the front or side of a building.

All the wall-mounted lights have their place in an outdoor lighting scheme—but if you want the best effects, use them carefully. Floodlights and the more powerful spotlights should be kept mainly for utilitarian lighting of drives, paths, yards and so on. But don't forget that patios and barbecue areas need utilitarian lighting too, so that you can see to cook safely. You may well be able to light these areas with judiciously-placed spotlights mounted on house walls. If you can direct the beam through trees or other foliage, to break up the light and provide it with a bit of colour, so much the better.

An alternative trick with spotlights is to mount them low, and shine them up at the house wall—though this may distort the architectural features of the house considerably, it will provide a much softer glow over a particular section of the garden.

Porch lights might provide some of your patio lighting—but be careful to place them where they will not cause glare. The type where the bulb is covered with multi-coloured glass panels might be more restful on the eyes than a clear glass globe—if the style goes well with your house.

Ground-fixed lights: To illuminate parts of your garden away from the house, the safest type of light to use is one that is securely fixed to the ground. One version consists of a steel spike with one or more spotlights mounted on top—you simply drive the spike into the ground wherever you want, and angle the light to illuminate a certain feature (usually a tree, hedge, or shrub). If you change your mind about siting it's easy to pull out the spike and stick it somewhere else (though moving the wiring may be more difficult—see below).

These spotlights are available either as *mains-voltage* or *low-voltage* types. The low-voltage type is based on sealed-beam car headlight lamps; they may be less flexible in beam spread and direction than the mains-voltage types, but they are very much safer and easier to wire (the cable can simply be laid along the ground) and changing their position in the garden is easy. Mains-voltage spotlights can be fitted with a variety of bulbs having different wattages (for varying levels of brightness), beam widths and so on. But wiring them up requires much more care, with the cable being buried well underground—and this makes it more awkward to move the lights once they have been installed.

Another type of light consists of a totally-enclosed and weatherproof bollard with a bulb mounted inside behind a translucent glass or plastic cover. These are part-buried in the ground and can be moved only with some upheaval, so you need to decide carefully first where you want them.

Often, a light mounted at ground level will be all you need in the garden itself—beams aimed upwards at trees and so on will be reflected back to ground level, and bollards, or spotlights aimed downwards, will light the ground sufficiently to make it possible to walk round the garden safely. Remember that you are not trying to create the levels of lighting that you would need inside the house.

If you do need bright illumination, however, you will have to mount a spotlight up high, and aim its beam down to ground level. Unless you have a sturdy brick wall nearby (in which case you can use any of the wall-mounted lights described above) it is best to use only low-voltage spotlights, for safety. These can be mounted on top of a pole or, for better looks, hidden in the upper branches of a nearby tree.

Festoons (or 'fairy lights) are sets of mains or low-wattage bulbs strung on a flex, and wound (carefully) through trees, along walls and so on. These are mainly for decoration, but of course, provide some illumination for lighting the tree and the surrounding ground as well.

Underwater lights: If you want to mount coloured lights in a pond or fountain use special low-voltage complete-sealed lamps.

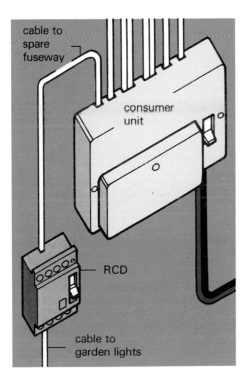

Locate the RCD near the point where the circuit is to enter the consumer unit

Providing protection

Whatever type of outdoor lighting you intend to install, protect the circuit with a **residual current device** (RCD), sometimes known as a current-operated earth-leakage circuit breaker (ELCB). This breaks the electric circuit if there is any leakage of current to earth which might cause an electric shock. An ordinary fuse or miniature circuit breaker (MCB) is not sufficient on its own—there are many potentially lethal faults it cannot react to, or won't react to quickly enough.

Use a high-sensitivity RCD fitted into just the outdoor circuit—it is easier to wire in this position, and means that if it trips by accident (as a high-sensitivity RCD sometimes does) it does not disrupt the electricity supply within the house.

Wiring an RCD into a circuit is usually easy—just a matter of connecting the ingoing and outgoing cables to the correctly-labelled terminals. It's best to locate the RCD at a point just before the cable enters the consumer unit.

Rigging up fairy lights

Fairy lights are often only temporary—wired up for a party, say. But it's just as important to make sure that they are safely installed as for a permanent installation.

There are two types of outdoor festoon lighting. One consists of a number of lamp-holders with miniature bulbs already

1 *Position the festoon lights on the special cable and press the cable over the pins. Seal up the ends of the cable with PVC tape*

2 *You can fit normal GLS 40W bulbs in many different colours to the lampholders to achieve a bright, decorative effect*

3 *Press the festoon cable through a hole drilled in the window frame or wall and seal the hole with mastic to prevent water penetrating*

4 *If the festoon lights are to be switched on from inside the house, the cable must have its own socket fitted with an RCD to protect the circuit*

prewired to a heavy-duty flex. The other consists of a special *festoon lampholder* which you fix to festoon cable. To assemble this sort, use a length of the cable specified by the manufacturers of the lamp-holders—usually 2.5mm² special festoon cable. Unscrew the top of the lampholder to expose the fixing pins beneath. Press the special cable over these pins so that one pin pierces the live core and the other pierces the neutral core, and screw the cap firmly back into place. Make sure the last lamp-holder on the circuit conceals the cut end of the cable. Separate the ends of the cable and wrap them with insulated PVC electricians' tape before closing the last lamp holder.

Although 2.5mm² cable can carry a great deal of current, it is wise to restrict the number of lamps to prevent too much voltage drop along its length. An absolute maximum of 40 lamps with a bulb rating of 40W is sensible.

Once you have made up a set of fairy lights, don't remove or reposition any of the lampholders—this will leave holes in the insulation which could let in water and cause a short circuit.

Hang your lights from trees, poles or buildings. Make sure the cable is not under tension and that none of the bulbs could swing against branches or walls—otherwise in a wind they could break, which would be very dangerous. Keep the bulbs high enough so that they are well out of people's reach.

Unless there is a special outdoor socket in your garden, you will have to plug your fairy lights into a socket in your house or outhouse. If the lights are going to be used for any length of time—perhaps over a summer holiday—it is worthwhile leading the free end of the flex into the house through a properly-made hole in the wall or in a window frame. Make the hole with a suitable drill, aiming to have it pointing downwards slightly towards the outside and large enough so that the flex will pass through without chafing. Seal up the hole both on the inside and the outside with a non-setting mastic.

Once inside the house, the flex can be wired to a plug. But don't plug this into an ordinary wall socket—instead, replace the nearest socket with a special socket-outlet fitted with its own high-sensitivity RCD and use only this for your lights.

If you have wired your festoon lights into special festoon cable, you will not be able to wire the end into an ordinary plug. In this instance you must wire the cable into a fused connection unit on a circuit fitted with an RCD for extra protection.

Connecting wall-mounted lights

Try to fix the light at about the level of the first floor—this will make wiring runs short and easy to install.

First drill a hole through the wall of the house—angling it slightly downwards towards the outside—large enough to take a piece of plastic conduit so that the cable will not chafe on the brickwork. If you are careful in positioning, the hole will fall between the floorboards and ceiling at the first floor level. Pass a length of 1mm² two-core and earth cable (*not* flex) through the hole and make the connections to the light. You may be connecting direct to the bulb holder, or to a connector inside the base of the light—if the latter, make sure the con-

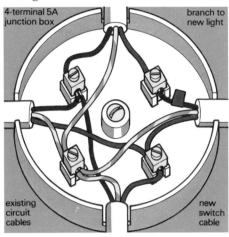

4-terminal 5A junction box

branch to new light

existing circuit cables

new switch cable

A junction box allows you to connect the new light and switch into the existing electricity supply

nections are housed inside a totally enclosed 'termination' box (if the light does not have one, you will have to add one). If the light is double-insulated, it will not need an earth connection, so you must cut back the earth wire to ensure it does not touch any part of the light. If the light is earthed, you must make sure the earth wire is properly connected to the right terminal.

Fasten the light to the wall, carefully sealing all joints and holes with mastic.

You can connect the feed cable to a switch and into the electricity supply in a number of ways. The easiest method is to break into the ground floor lighting circuit and insert a joint box as shown in the diagram, connecting to it both the feed cable from the outside light and the cable going to the switch.

If the wall light is set at a low level, drill through the wall in the same way and take

5 *By removing the back of a low-voltage spotlight it can simply be 'threaded' onto the low-voltage cable supplied*

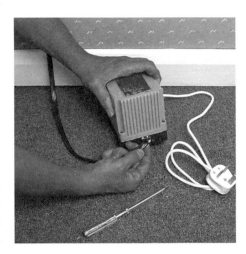

6 *Cable from any low-voltage lights must be connected to a specified transformer before being plugged into the RCD socket*

7 *Push the mounting spike well into the ground. One or more spotlights provide intense decorative lighting among shrubbery*

your supply from the ring main via a 5 amp fused connection unit.

Providing the lights, and any external cables, are kept out of reach there is no real need to fit an RCD to this sort of circuit.

Connecting a bollard away from the house follows exactly the same procedure except that you will have to dig a trench for the supply as you would for any mains-voltage garden fixture.

Installing low-voltage lights

Although low-voltage lights are not electrically dangerous, you still need to exercise some care when installing them.

You can place low-voltage lights anywhere you like in the garden and simply run cables back to the house from each, or you may be able to run several lights off the same cable. Remember that you will need relatively thicker cable to cope with the low voltage—a 40W bulb running at 12 volts takes 3.3 amps, compared to the 0.16 amps a 40W bulb at 240 volts takes, and it is current-carrying capacity that determines the thickness of a cable. The manufacturer's instuctions will explain what is needed. One of the advantages of such lights is that you do not need to bury or protect the cable. But once you have decided exactly where you want your lights it is wise to do so—cutting through the cable is at best irritating, and will probably blow fuses or trip protecting devices in the circuit's transformer. Lay the cables at the bottom of a trench about 500mm deep, on top of a bed of sand—it isn't essential to protect the cable in conduit or with paving slabs as for mains-voltage supplies.

Pass the cables into the house through a hole drilled in the wall, and then seal the opening inside and out. Connect the ends to a transformer. Again, follow manufacturer's instructions on this—they will specify what type of transformer is necessary and how large it needs to be for the number of lights you want.

Connecting mains-voltage garden lights

Mains-voltage lights in the garden may provide you with the best lighting display, but they are the most difficult to wire up.

You must run a separate circuit from the consumer unit to a socket (or sockets) in the garden, and this circuit must be protected by an RCD. Decide where your light is going to be placed and drive a sturdy post,

8 *Drive a sturdy post into the ground where you want the light and wire up a 13 amp weatherproof socket*

9 *Protect the cable along its run in heavy duty plastic conduit. Bury the cable in a trench at least 500mm deep*

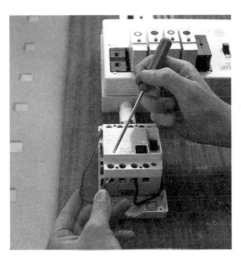

10 *Protect the circuit with a high sensitivity RCD which will break the circuit if there is any current leakage*

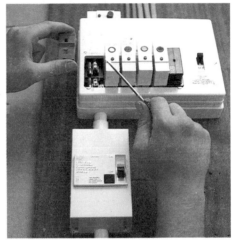

11 *Wire the circuit into a spare fuseway in the consumer unit or a swiched fuse unit linked to the meter*

pressure-impregnated with preservative, firmly into the ground. Fix to this a 13 amp weatherproof socket, mounted on a plastic conduit box. You can, if you wish, include a weathertight switch at this point—but make sure it has a rating of 15A or more. Plan the circuit in the same way as you would an ordinary indoor lighting circuit beginning at the point farthest from the consumer unit and working back to it by the most direct run.

From your post, dig a trench across the garden (at least 500mm deep, and as narrow as you can make it) to the house at a point close to the consumer unit. Connect a length of 2.5mm² two-core and earth cable to the garden socket and, protecting it in heavy duty plastic conduit all the way from the conduit box to within the house, lay it in the trench on a bed of sand for protection.

Before you backfill the trench it is essential that you cover the cable with special tiles marked 'electric live cable' along the entire length of the run as a precaution against someone accidentally cutting through the cable while digging in the garden. With the tiles in place, fill in the trench and compact it. Continue the cable run inside the house in the normal way until it reaches the consumer unit.

Here fit a 15 amp high-sensitivity (30mA) RCD into the wall and wire the supply cable to it, following the manufacturer's instructions. Connect the RCD in turn (still using 2.5mm² cable) to a spare fuseway in the consumer unit, protected by a 15 amp fuse or MCB. If there is no spare fuseway, connect the RCD to a new switched fuse unit (fused at 20 amps) and get the electricity board to connect this.

CHAPTER 4

BATHROOM ELECTRICS

Electrical installations in the bathroom have to be treated with extra caution because of the dangers of steam or water getting into the components. But approach the problem in the correct manner and a range of fittings, including heaters and shaver units, can be installed successfully

FIT A WALL HEATER

Wall heaters are the ideal solution for rooms which are used intermittently—such as bathrooms. You turn the heater on only for as long as you need it and, because they are radiant, as opposed to convection heaters, they warm you rather than everything else in the room.

Fitting a wall heater is easy but, because you can't have an electrical socket in the bathroom, you can't just plug one in. Don't worry, all you have to do is take off a spur from your power circuit and wire the heater into that via a fused connection unit.

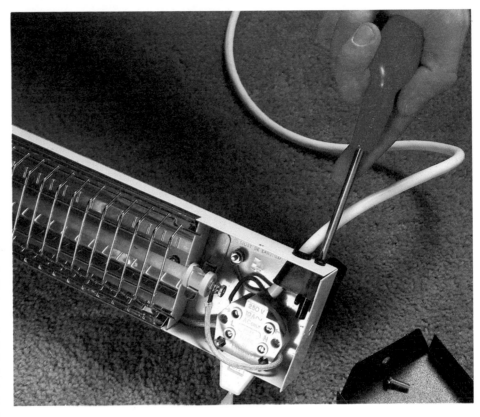

Choosing a wall heater

Wall heaters are readily available and inexpensive so it's worth going for a neat design which will blend with your bathroom decor.

If you are installing a wall heater in a bathroom it must be unswitched or have an integral cord operated switch—it's unsafe to have ordinary switches in a moist atmosphere and this is prohibited by wiring regulations. Some heaters have their pull switch in the middle, others at the side. If you use an unswitched model, it must be controlled by a switch fitted outside the bathroom—a very inconvenient option—or by a separate pullcord operated switch introduced into the circuit. In either case, you are likely to have much more cable routing to do—so choose a switched heater if at all possible.

Sizes for the most powerful types of wall heater are around 700mm to 800mm long with a depth of up to 200mm. You can buy them with ratings of between 750 watts and 1kW for single element models—double that for double element heaters. The size generally increases with the power rating.

Which kind you choose will depend on your preferences about appearance—and on how warm you want to be—but a 1kW heater is sufficient to warm up the average small bathroom.

Planning

As always when installing any electrical equipment—especially in a bathroom—safety should be your prime consideration. Check the following points before you start:
Siting the heater: The important thing to remember about positioning a wall heater in

a bathroom is that it must be impossible to touch while you are using any of the taps or when you are having a bath or shower. High up on the wall opposite the bath is the

best position. Of course, it shouldn't be so high that you can't reach the cord.
Wiring: The heater should be wired up with 0.75mm² three-core sheathed flex to

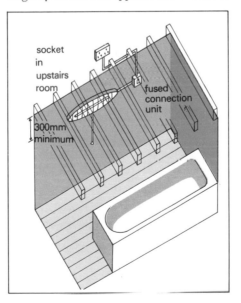

The ideal situation is to borrow power from a socket in the room above. Don't put the heater above the bath or too near the ceiling

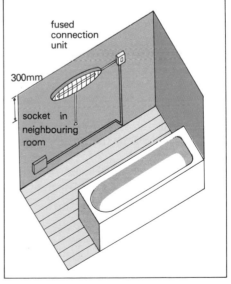

It's more likely you'll have to wire up the fused connection unit to a socket next door which means a longer cable run to the heater

an adjacent fused connector unit which is then connected with 2.5mm² twin-and-earth electric cable to the back of a nearby socket. The only complicated part is deciding on the route of the cable and which socket to use. You have the choice of running the cable in the wall or of using surface mounted mini-trunking. However, the first thing to do is to find out which socket you can wire up to.

So that there is no danger of you overloading your circuit, start by working out if it's a ring or radial type; it may affect whether or not you can install a heater. If you don't already know, investigate by examining a number of your sockets in the following way. Turn off the electricity at the mains. Unscrew three or four socket outlets from their mounting boxes and look at the wiring: a ring main socket will have two sets of cable attached to it, a radial circuit will have only one. However, some radial circuits have several sockets strung together so you may find two cables attached to any one socket. Similarly, some ring circuits have spurs extending from them. If you open up one of these, you will see only one cable. The answer is to look at three or four sockets to establish a general pattern.

Once you have established which type of circuit you have, the rule is that on a radial, use a socket which has only one cable leading to it, and on a ring, use a socket which has two cables leading to it.

★ WATCH POINT ★

If you find three cables attached to your socket it means that somebody has already taken a spur from it to power a new installation so you will need to try another one.

Locating the best socket: The socket you select should be chosen not only for its electrical suitability but also for convenience in terms of routing the cable. The shorter the distance, the less work you will have to do—so it's well worth spending a little time planning the layout before starting work.

The ideal is a two gang socket in a room directly above the bathroom, because you can then run the cable straight downwards for a short distance—a relatively simple job. However, the chances are that your bathroom is on the top floor. If so, pick a socket in the next door room. Whatever your choice, you will have to make a hole for the cable, either through the wall or ceiling.

★ WATCH POINT ★

Try to connect to a double gang socket because there will be more space in its mounting box for the extra cable than in a single socket box.

Routing the cable: There is one golden rule to follow: the runs must be vertical and horizontal—never diagonal. You have a choice of two methods of routing the cable so that it is protected—either in a surface mounted conduit or concealed in a channel. **Surface mounted conduit** can be used on any type of wall—it is the easiest method of running cable. You can make it less obtrusive by careful routing and by painting it to match the walls or skirting.

Concealed routing is neater and gives you two options depending on your wall construction. You can tell the type of wall by tapping it with the handle of a screwdriver: a solid and fairly flat thump indicates a plastered masonry wall, a hollow sound means a timber frame wall. On a masonry wall, you can channel out a groove which can be filled and redecorated; on a timber frame wall, you can drop the cable behind the plasterboard.

Additional materials

You will certainly need to have a fused connection unit—choose an unswitched type fitted with a 13A fuse—a surface mounting box to fit it, a sufficient length of 2.5mm² twin-and-earth cable and 0.75mm² three core sheathed flex, cable clips, rubber grommets—which protect the cable in the mounting boxes—and yellow/green earth sleeving.

And, depending on how you decide to fix the cable, you may need plastic conduit, 25mm No. 8 wood screws plus wallplugs and cellulose filler.

Tools for the job

The only essential tools are an electrician's screwdriver, spirit level, drill and bits and a trimming knife. For cutting conduit, a hacksaw is useful and, if you are channelling out a groove in a masonry wall, a bolster and club hammer will be handy. You need decorating equipment to make good any channels when the job is done.

Routing the cable

Once you have decided on the cable route, mark it onto the wall together with the position of the heater and its connection unit.

Make a final check to see that both the heater and unit can be securely fastened to the wall and that the marks are level. You don't need to channel in the flex from the heater to the unit, but mount them close together to keep it short.

Fix the surface mounting box for the connection unit to the wall using impact adhesive (if the wall surface is sufficiently sound) or wall fastenings and screws. Measure and cut the channelling for the mini-trunking and fix it to the wall.

At your chosen break-through point, use a 10mm masonry bit to make a neat hole for

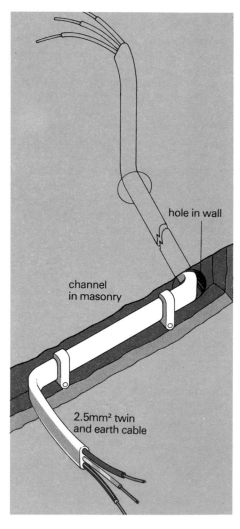

hole in wall

channel in masonry

2.5mm² twin and earth cable

In a masonry wall conceal the cable in a channel. Secure it with a cable clips and plaster over later. Drill a hole straight through the wall at a convenient point for breaking into the supply

the cable to go through the wall. Prepare the cable route to the socket by cutting a channel to the socket and entering its box from the side or by threading the cable through from behind and up the plasterboard, or by using conduit.

Push the cable through the hole in the wall and take it to the socket. Then feed the cable into the channelling securing it with clips every 100mm or so and through to the back of the connection unit mounting box. Make sure that there is enough cable at both ends to allow for the odd mistake in cutting or wire stripping—and for working on the ends of the wires.

It's convenient at this stage to connect the end of the cable to the fused connection unit: It isn't necessary to turn off the power while you do this—you won't be connecting to any live wires until everything else is

1 *Decide the position of the heater—not over the bath and more than 300mm from the ceiling—and mark onto the wall*

2 *Fix the connection unit mounting box to the wall close to the position of the heater so the connecting flex will be short*

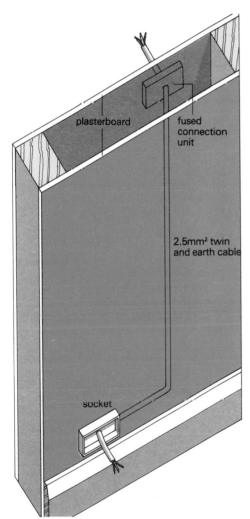

In a timber frame wall you can run the cable through the cavity although you may have to pass it through some timbers by drilling holes, or cutting out notches (see page 27)

3 *Drill through the wall at a convenient point for connecting in to the socket. If you are drilling close to the socket be very careful not to drill into a live wire. If you don't know where the wires go, switch off and make a hole by hand with a cold chisel*

wired up. But don't under any circumstances try to connect the cable to the socket that you are drawing power from at this stage—you **must** turn off the power before doing so.

Connecting to the fused connection unit. Thread the end of the cable through the most conveniently positioned knockout panel in the connection unit mounting box and fit a grommet. Cut the cable to a convenient length and strip back the outer sheathing by about 75mm. Remove about 10mm of insulation from the wires and slip a yellow/green sleeve over the bare earth.

Insert the wires into their terminals in the connection unit. The unit will have

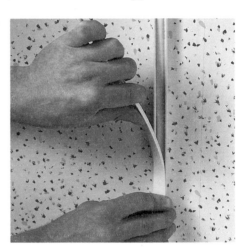

4 *Surface mounted conduit avoids the need for any further holes in the wall*

5 *Connect the supply cable to the correct terminals on the feed side of the unit*

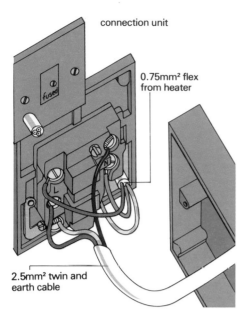

connection unit

0.75mm² flex from heater

fused

2.5mm² twin and earth cable

6 Wire up the heater flex to the correct terminals in the heater and refit the cover

7 Lead the flex into the front of the unit and connect to the terminals on the load side

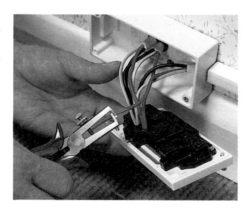

8 Switch off the mains, then connect the supply cable to the back of the chosen socket

The connection unit has two sets of terminals for the supply cable (feed) and heater flex (load). The flex outlet has a flex clamp to prevent straining the lead to the heater. Fit a 13A fuse

separate live and neutral terminals for the mains cable (labelled feed) and for the flex leading to the heater (labelled load). The earth terminal is common to both (see right). Connect the red wire to the live (L) terminal on the feed side and the black wire to the neutral (N) terminal. When you've done this, connect the sleeved earth wire to the earth terminal.

Fixing the heater

With the fused connection wired up you can now fix the heater to the wall. Working overhead is awkward so get help.

Hold the heater up against its marks and adjust its position.

Mark the position of the fixing holes with a pencil and drill the wall for the fixings. Use the same type of plugs as you used for the connection unit box.

Cut the heater flex to length allowing some extra for connection, strip back about 75mm of the outer sheath and 20mm of the insulation from the three wires and connect them up to the terminals in the heater. The brown wire goes to the live (L) terminal, the blue to the neutral (N) and the green/yellow to the earth terminal. You may also need to fit the element to its screw terminals.

With the heater on its marks, screw through the fixing brackets into the wall fixings. Adjust the angle of the heater so that it will radiate diagonally down into the room. You might have to adjust this later.

With the fused connection unit faceplate unscrewed from the mounting box, loosen the flex clamp, slip the flex through it, strip the end and fix the wires into their terminals. The brown heater flex wire goes into the live (L) load terminal corresponding with the red spur cable in the live feed

terminal, the blue heater wire into the neutral (N) load terminal corresponding with the black spur wire in the neutral feed terminal and the yellow/green earth wire with the yellow/green sleeved earth wire of the spur cable to the earthing screw. Tighten up the flex clamp making sure that it grips the outer sheath of the heater flex. Fit a 13 amp fuse and screw the plate back on to the mounting box.

★ WATCH POINT ★

As the heater is near the ceiling and many ceilings often aren't quite level, it may be better to align with the ceiling rather than against a spirit level.

Connecting the power

With the heater fixed up and all the wiring connections made inside the bathroom you can make the final connection to the power supply.

Before you attempt to do this **you must ensure that the electricity is switched off at the mains.** With this done you can unscrew the faceplate of the socket and pull it forward out of the way.

Feed the end of the cable through an appropriate knock-out panel in the box and fit a protective grommet.

Cut the cable to the same length as the existing wiring and strip back about 75mm of the outer sheathing and about 10mm of insulation from the red and black wires. Don't forget to slip a length of yellow/green sleeving on the bare earth wire.

Unscrew the terminals at the back of the faceplate and insert the new wires. Connect the red wire into the live (L) terminal and the black into the neutral (N) terminal. Connect up the earth wire to the earth plate at the side.

Replace the faceplate and any conduit cover strips, turn the power back on then test the heater. If it doesn't operate properly, switch off at the mains and re-check all your connections.

Finishing off

If you have used surface mounted conduit, there is unlikely to be any making good to do. But if you have channelled the wires you will have to fill over them and then redecorate.

INSTALL A SHAVER UNIT

For those who use an electric razor, it's unfortunate that it isn't just a simple matter of plugging the device into the most convenient three-pin socket outlet. Instead, it has to be operated from a special point which will accept the continental-style two-pin plug that is invariably moulded onto the end of its flex.

Rather than installing a proper outlet unit, you may be tempted to buy a three-pin socket converter. But at best this can only be a temporary measure. You still won't be able to use the razor in the bathroom—you aren't allowed any sockets there—and in other rooms most sockets will be at floor level, which means that if you use the razor standing up in front of a mirror, then the flex could well be over-strained. Sooner or later you'll find it makes sense to install a proper shaver outlet unit, or units, which are permanently connected to the fixed wiring of the house.

Types of shaver outlet

Outlet units come in several forms and the terminology used to describe them sometimes varies among the manufacturers. What you must be aware of, though, is that there's one type that can be used in any room, including bathrooms and cloakrooms, and another, which must not be used in a bathroom. So when you go to buy a shaver socket, make doubly sure you get the right one.

The reason for having two types has to do with the UK IEE wiring regulations regarding the use of appliances in bathrooms (and in cloakrooms with showers); the regulations are geared to making it impossible for you to touch anything electric since there's always a chance that you'll have wet hands.

This is where the shaver outlet unit approved for bathroom use comes into its own: it contains a double-pole isolating transformer and the outlet supply is taken from the secondary winding, which is effectively separated from the earthed mains supply. This safety feature eliminates the risk of getting a shock in a 'wet environment' and also prevents anything but a razor from being powered by the outlet.

Shaver outlet units without a transformer are naturally cheaper, but they're definitely

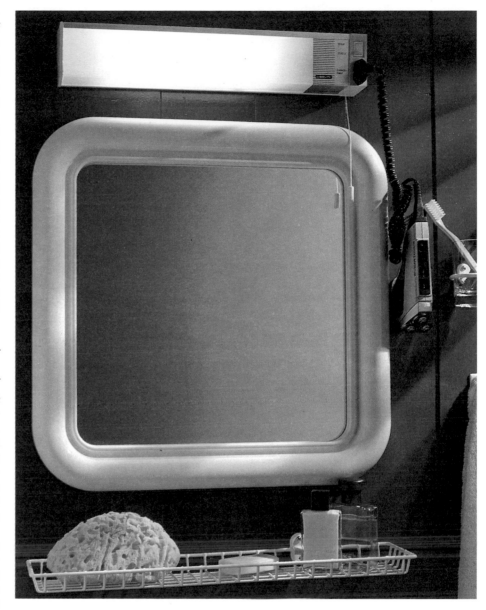

not safe if there's any chance of them being touched by wet hands.

Fitting a shaver socket and light

If you plan to install a shaver outlet in a bathroom, then it's well worth considering using one that also includes a light in a neat casing. From a practical point of view, bathroom lighting is often far from satisfactory —a central, close-mounted and encased fitting being the norm, with many fittings taking nothing more than a 60W bulb. For most of the time you're in the bathroom

you tend to stand with your back to this light, so washing, shaving or applying make-up are done in your own shadow. With a shaver socket/light unit fitted over a mirror you'll be able to get round this problem by providing excellent, close-quarters illumination.

Outwardly, all these units look similar, consisting of a tubular lamp and a socket—either at one end or underneath—for the razor. The light works independently of the socket and is operated by a short pull-cord switch. Some units use a small fluorescent tube with a 15W, 20W or 30W rating, while others use a 60W tungsten filament striplight. These lamps are nearly always

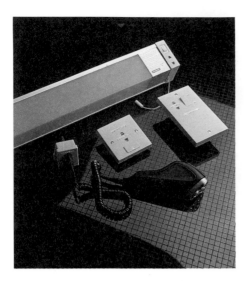

Four types of shaver socket. Only the two largest, each fitted with an isolating transformer, are suitable for use in bathrooms

covered by a diffuser, which spreads the light evenly and stops discomforting glare from the mirror.

Safety is the keynote with these units and nothing is left to chance. For example, even without a diffuser, special shields prevent you from touching the live parts of the lampholders when changing the fluorescent tube or striplight. In fact, as an added precaution the power to the light is often automatically cut off as the diffuser is lifted out or you start to turn the fluorescent tube to remove it.

Another point to look at on these units is the socket outlet itself. Some units have what's known as a dual-voltage facility, which means they can accommodate razors that run off 115 volts as well as those running on the standard European 230–250 volts. The socket on this type of unit has three holes arranged in a line, the centre hole being common to both voltages. Note that the safety shutters on the holes operate the on/off mechanism; when the razor plug is inserted, the power automatically comes on—there's no separate switch as there is on other units.

Standard shaver outlet units

If you're happy with your lighting, or if the mirror you shave at extends well above head height, you might as well install a straight-forward shaver supply unit. These, too, are available with dual voltage facilities, the required voltage being determined by the

flick of a switch rather than the selection of the appropriate holes on the socket panel. (In fact, these are the only rocker switches that are allowed in a bathroom.) There's also a separate on/off switch.

The best place to site such a unit is probably at chest height and to one side of your shaving mirror.

All the units mentioned so far contain transformers and are therefore intended primarily for bathroom or cloakroom use—although this doesn't exclude them from being used elsewhere in the home. However, the fact that the units without transformers are cheaper makes them attractive alternatives for bedroom use. They also tend to be smaller, with less obtrusive faceplates, so they aren't such a conspicuous feature next to, say, a dressing table or dress mirror. Such outlets are protected by a 1 amp or 2 amp fuse and they, too, contain a thermal overload device to restrict their use to shavers.

Power supply

Finding a power source for a shaver socket is not difficult. For the types incorporating an isolating transformer and thermal overload device, you can take the power from the lighting circuit, the power circuit or a junction box linked to the power circuit.

If you are installing the shaver socket in your bathroom, it's probably easiest to take the power from that room's lighting circuit as the nearest power socket will certainly be outside the room. All you need to do is fit a three-way junction box close to a lighting cable (the 1.00mm² size), switch the power off and make the connections.

When taking the power from a power circuit, you can either take it direct from a socket or fit a junction box into the nearest power cable. Once again, however, always check that the power is off.

In all cases, double check your wiring before turning the power on again.

Shaver sockets not incorporating an isolating transformer must be wired via a fused connection unit and must never be installed in a bathroom.

If you're taking the power direct from a power socket, this calls for some care in organising your wiring. From the power socket to the fused connection unit, run 2.5mm² cable, but from the connection unit to the shaver socket, you must use the lower rating 1.00mm² cable.

To ensure that this has proper fuse protection, you need to fit the fused connection unit with a 3 amp fuse.

Tools and materials

In all cases, screwdrivers, wire strippers, a trimming knife and an electric drill with bits are essential items (note that for drilling through ceramic tiles you'll need a spear point bit). You're also certain to need a supply of wall fixings and screws.

For flush installations, have a club hammer, sharp bolster and cold chisel to hand, plus a bag of plaster for making good.

If you decide on surface mounting, you'll need plastic conduit (mini trunking) together with a means of fixing it—screws, masonry pins or impact adhesive.

Electrical connections to the shaver unit are made using 1.00mm² PVC sheathed two core and earth lighting cable. If you're wiring into the lighting circuit, you will also need a three way junction box and cable clips.

If your shaver unit has a transformer and you're wiring it on a direct spur from the main power circuit, buy 2.5mm² cable. Non-transformer units must be wired in 1.00mm² cable as far as a 3 amp fused connection unit and then on to the power circuits in 2.55m².

Fitting the unit

First decide exactly where the unit is to go and mark its position on the wall. From here onwards the procedure may vary depending on whether the cable and unit are flush or surface mounted.

If you're wiring into the lighting circuit, mark out the cable drop from the ceiling, using a plumbline to get a true vertical. Then push a bradawl into the junction of the ceiling and the wall on the proposed route to check that it isn't obstructed by a joist. Now bore a hole in the ceiling at your chosen point.

If the cable is to be surface mounted, cut a run of plastic conduit to stretch from the unit to the point where the cable enters the room and fix the back section to the wall.

For flush mounting, mark out the edges of a cable channel 18mm–25mm wide and also the recess for the unit's backing box with a sharp bolster chisel. Cut out the channel and recess, using both the bolster and a cold chisel to a depth of at least 38mm, then square off the sides.

Feed the cable through its entry point into the room. At the unit, allow about 150mm extra for connections at this end. Place the cable in its conduit and clip on the cover or lay it in the channel and replaster.

On a conventional shaver unit, lay the backing box against the wall and mark the fixing holes. Drill these to take plugs or cavity fixings as necessary.

On a combined light/socket unit, remove the diffuser and take out the lamp. Underneath there will either be fixing holes, or screws holding the body of the unit to its mounting bracket. Having gained access to the holes, place a spirit level on the unit to check that it is horizonal then mark their positions on the wall. Drill and plug the holes to take the appropriate fixings.

On a conventional unit, fit a rubber grommet to the cable entry hole, feed in the cable and screw the unit to the wall. On a light unit, check that the cable feeds in neatly through the entry point on the backing plate as you screw it home.

Connecting the power

If you're breaking into the lighting circuit in the roof space, finding an appropriate cable should be easy. At first floor level, you may have to raise a few floorboards before you track one down.

Lighting cables are going to be the only cables running in your roof space, so all you need do is select the one passing closest to the bathroom. Depending on how the wiring is arranged, you may need to lift some insulation to follow its route, so a pair of gloves will come in handy especially if your skin is sensitive to glass fibre.

If you have any doubts about a particular cable being part of the lighting circuit, simply trace its path. The cable should lead you to a ceiling rose. If you don't come to a ceiling rose quickly, find the nearest rose you can and then determine whether any of its cables will be suitable for your purposes.

If you are breaking into the lighting circuit running between the ground floor ceiling and the first floor, don't simply lift floorboards at random. The chances are that this will be awkward anyway—the degree of difficulty depending on the type of floor covering you have. Before you lift any boards, make sure you know where the nearest ceiling rose is.

Start wiring up at the unit end. Strip back the sheathing of the cable and then strip about 6mm of insulation from the live and neutral cores. The exposed earth core should be sheathed in green/yellow PVC tube. Connect the three cores to their appropriate terminals, following the maker's instructions. On some units you may find a two-part terminal block, to make the wiring easier.

1 *Begin wiring up by stripping back the cable's outer sheathing and about 6mm of insulation from the live and neutral cores*

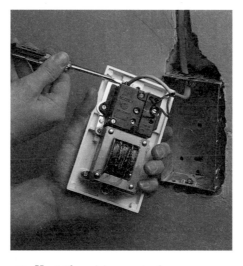

2 *Connect the wires to their appropriate terminals. Do not forget to sheath the exposed earth core in green/yellow plastic tubing*

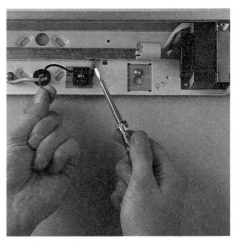

3 *Keep the wiring neat when connecting to a flush unit. Slack wiring may get nipped by the backing box*

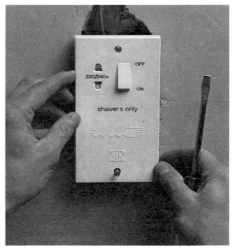

4 *With the connections completed, screw on the faceplate, check that it is level and then make good the chase*

5 *If the fitting includes a strip light, complete the wiring, fit the bulb in place and then position the diffuser*

6 *Run the supply cable for the shaver socket to the lighting cable. Secure the new cable with clips at regular intervals*

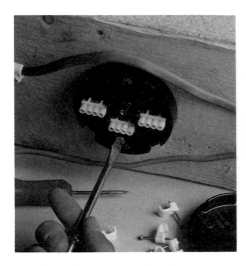

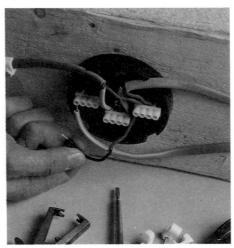

7 *Fit a three way junction box to the joist in the most suitable position for your connections; then check that the power is off*

8 *Cut the lighting cable and connect it to the junction box terminals. You then simply connect the shaver socket supply cable*

On a conventional unit, complete this end of the job by screwing on the faceplate and checking that it is switched off.

On a combined light unit, refit the body or cover, followed by the lamp and then the diffuser.

Finding a power source for a shaver socket is not difficult. For the types incorporating an isolating transformer and thermal overload device, you can take the power from the lighting circuit, the power circuit or a junction box linked to the power circuit

junction box connected to lighting circuit

shaver socket with isolating transformer

existing socket

junction box

isolating transformer

At this stage turn off the electricity supply at the main switch and remove the fuse from the circuit on which you'll be working. Remember that you'll need a torch if you're making the connections in the dark recesses of a roof space.

Note that the instructions given here are for breaking into a lighting circuit; taking a spur from a ring or radial power circuit is covered in detail on pages 74–77. For a shaver unit, you have three basic choices when connecting into a power circuit. For units fitted with an isolating transformer, you can take the power directly from the mains circuit using 2.5mm^2 cable. To do this, you can either run cable to the back of an existing socket and connect in (see the diagram below left), or you can fit a junction box into an existing power cable and take the power from there. For units without an isolating transformer, you'll need to run 1.0mm^2 cable to a fused connection unit and then 2.5mm^2 cable onto the power circuit.

Clip the cable neatly to the joists as far as the break-in point on the existing power supply cable. When you reach it, screw a three way junction box to the nearest adjacent joist, then strip and prepare the cable as you did at the unit end.

Plan your location for the junction box carefully. Strictly speaking, it's not advisable to bury cables and junction boxes beneath insulation, as the materials may allow excess heat to build up. If you've fitted the minimum recommended depth of insulation, then screwing a junction box to the side of a joist may not be possible without partially covering it. The answer is to fit the junction box between joists using a batten.

To accommodate a junction box comfortably, you'll need at least a 75mm × 25mm batten and two 25mm × 25mm offcuts to use as joint blocks at either end. Screw the offcuts to the joists, and then screw the batten to the offcuts. Fit the junction box to the batten and then carry on with your wiring. The main point to note with this method is that you may need to reroute some of the existing cable slightly. If the existing cable is held in place with clips, remove some and check to see if there is enough slack or flexibility in the route to allow you to pass the existing cable close to the new junction box.

Connect all three sets of wires to their appropriate terminals in the junction box, exactly as shown in the diagram left. Check that the terminals are right and refit the junction box cover. You are now ready to reinstate the supply and test the unit.

CHAPTER 5

ALARMS, BELLS AND CONTROLS

A burglar alarm or door answering system could help make your home and its contents safe and secure. They are easy to install and electrical connections are straightforward. Central heating controls can also help you monitor the efficiency of your heating system—and save money at the same time

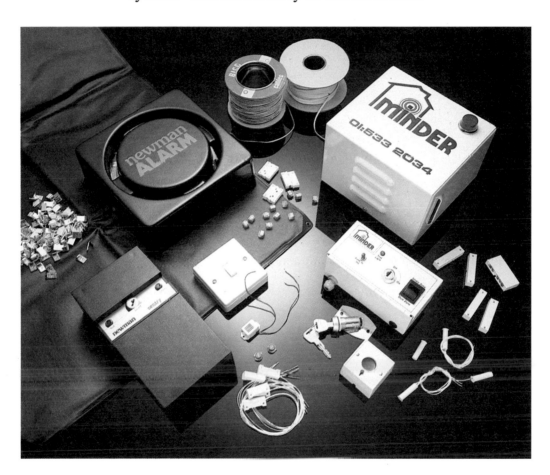

BURGLAR ALARM

Your first line of defence against intrusion into your home should be strong door locks and lockable window fastenings. But a good burglar alarm is the best deterrent. With modern electronics they have become increasingly sophisticated and harder for burglars to defeat; which has meant a consequent increase in the security of your home.

Burglar alarm systems

Most systems consist of the following:

A control unit: This incorporates the on/off switch and sets off the alarm when one of the sensors detects an intruder. Many incorporate an automatic delay so that you can activate the system, then leave the house through a door on which a sensor is mounted without setting off the alarm.

An alarm unit: This usually consists of a bell or siren mounted in a box and fitted on a

prominent part of an outside wall as a visual deterrent. The alarm (like the control unit) is battery operated so that power cuts don't deactivate it, and is fitted with an anti-tamper device so that any attempt to move or destroy it sets off the alarm.

Sensor units: There are usually two types —magnetic sensors fitted to doors and windows, and pressure pads which are laid under carpets on the likely path of an intruder as he moves through the house. A third, but less common, type of sensor is the infra-red movement sensor. This works a little like radar, detecting movement in a darkened room to set off the alarm. It is less common in DIY installations, but frequently found in professional systems protecting commercial premises.

Wiring: Most wiring consists of two core flex running between the various components of the system, but it is possible to get anti-tamper wiring which sets off the alarm when cut or bridged.

For obvious reasons, many technical details are revealed only in the manufacturer's instructions. Your choice of alarm system depends very much on your requirements, and you are advised to shop around, consulting manufacturers before deciding which system is best. However, except in the most unusual circumstances, there is little to choose between many of the DIY systems.

Preparation and planning

Whatever system you decide on, you must read the instructions carefully and familiarize yourself completely with all the component parts.

Draw a plan of your home to decide where the alarm's sensors—magnetic or pressure pad devices—should be located. Choose where the control unit is to go—in general it should be sited as close to your front door as possible so that you can prime or switch off the system on leaving or entering the house without the alarm going off (though not all systems work in this way). Locate the siren where it can be seen and heard. If you fit it to an outside wall where the sound will be muffled by a tall hedge or outbuilding, you'll lose not only the sound of the siren but also the visual deterrent that sirens provide.

Where valuables are kept in a particular room fit a combination of alarm sensors and stout locks. Remember also that a burglar will generally enter a house by the easiest and least observable route so that is where adequate alarm protection is most needed.

The picture opposite shows a typical layout for an alarm system in a two-storey house. The siren should be mounted high up on an outside wall, and prominently positioned to serve as a deterrent to would-be burglars. The wiring from the control unit passes through the wall in to the back of the siren, leaving nothing exposed and vulnerable. The system's control unit is concealed under the stairs where it is within easy reach of the front door. The sensor on the front door is part of the entry/exit circuit so that it is possible to enter or leave the house without the alarm sounding when it is switched on. The rest of the sensors are divided between two zones: zone 1 is downstairs, zone 2 is upstairs. They can be switched on and off independently to protect part of the house while the family are in another part. The 'panic button' is mounted beside the bed and activates the siren whether the alarm system is switched on or not.

Tools for the job

You will need a power or hand drill, a 19mm flat drill bit for recessed contacts, a 4mm wood twist drill, No. 10 masonry drill bit, screwdrivers, a sharp chisel, tack hammer, pliers, wire strippers, and, in some circumstances, a long masonry drill bit to bring wires through external cavity walls. In addition to any of the tools you don't have and the kit itself, you will probably also need to buy the appropriate gauge of wiring for interconnection (the instructions will detail this), batteries, cable clips, and pins.

Test the system

Test the major components of the alarm system before attempting installation. This serves a dual purpose—it will enable you to ensure that all the equipment is working correctly and also gives you a chance to familiarize yourself with the components.

Follow the maker's instructions for the connection of batteries and temporary disconnection of the anti-tamper device, if necessary, and then go through each of the specified test procedures as instructed. This way you can be sure that the system will only actuate in 'anger'.

Installing the control unit and siren

The control unit is the heart of the burglar alarm system and controls all its functions.

Site the control unit in a convenient position close to the main exit of your home or wherever the instructions specify. Understair cupboards often provide ideal locations.

Using a masonry bit, drill into the wall at the planned position, plug the holes with wall plugs and screw the back plate to the wall.

Fit the siren on an external wall out of a potential burglar's reach but as close to the control unit as possible. Often this means high up on a front wall close to the eaves.

Ideally, you should run the cable used for connecting the control unit to the siren up through the interior of the house and feed it through the wall directly into the siren.

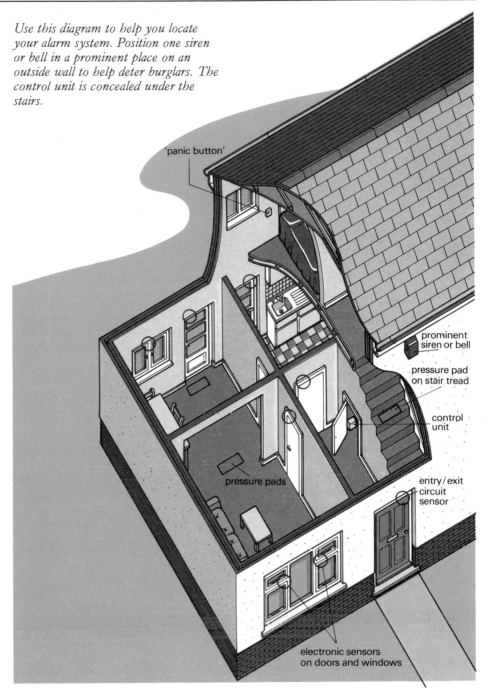

Use this diagram to help you locate your alarm system. Position one siren or bell in a prominent place on an outside wall to help deter burglars. The control unit is concealed under the stairs.

'panic button'

prominent siren or bell

pressure pad on stair tread

control unit

pressure pads

entry/exit circuit sensor

electronic sensors on doors and windows

Follow the maker's instructions closely for this part of the installation as the siren unit will probably include a number of fail-safe and other anti-tamper devices.

With both control unit and siren in position, the two units can be connected.

Wiring

Route all cabling as inconspicuously as possible. Cable can be hidden behind skirting boards, channelled into walls or run under carpets. Ensure that you make good electrical connections—the alarm will fail otherwise.

Measure the length of cable you need—allow a little extra for errors—to make a neat job. Normally 0.5 amp two-core cable is required—this is available at most electrical or hardware stores.

Route the cabling as appropriate between the sensor and the control box. Make sure that enough cable is left to make a connection to the terminals easily.

Use wire strippers to bare the cable. Remove about 5mm of insulation material from each core.

Decide on your major exit/entry route. Normally this will be the front door, but any external door is appropriate. Do not place pressure pads on this route. Normally the

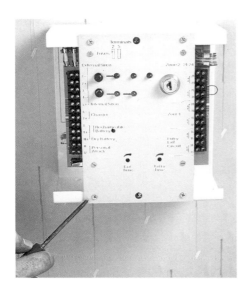

1 *Having bench-tested the system, fit the control unit, preferably out of sight and close to the main entrance of the house*

2 *Fit the siren in a prominent spot high up on the outside wall. Try to run the wire straight into it through the wall— leave none exposed*

3 *Make the connections according to the manufacturer's instructions and remember to fit any batteries which are required at this stage*

time allowed for opening and closing the exit door after the control unit is switched on is about thirty seconds, so make sure you can reach the door and leave in that space of time. Not all alarms use this system, how-ever, so check with the manufacturer's instructions beforehand.

Some manufacturers supply 4-core cable for their systems which can be fitted in such a way that cutting it sets off the alarm. Most do not specify which colours of core should be used for which connection—to foil thieves—so choose for yourself, but make a note somewhere for reference in case problems should arise.

Magnetic sensors

Basically these sensors are magnetic switches that will detect if a window or door is opened or closed. The switch assembly consists of two parts—the switch itself, which you fit to the window or door frame, and the magnetic actuator, which goes on the door or opening window. The gap between the two sections should not be greater than 6mm when the door or window is closed.

Hide the sensors from view. An ideal location is at the top of doors and windows.

Using a suitable drill bit or chisel, cut or drill into the centre of the door or window frame edge to a sufficient depth to house the sensor comfortably.

Repeat the process on the fixed frames but add a little more depth to allow for the passage of the cable.

If a flush fit is needed, you will have to chisel away sufficient framework to allow for the sensor flange.

For hidden cables you will need to drill through the outer or upper edge of the fixed frames into the hole previously cut to locate the sensor.

Surface sensors can also be obtained.

4 *Conceal the wiring. Run it under carpets, behind skirting boards and tuck it into the angle of door frames but make sure it cannot get trapped*

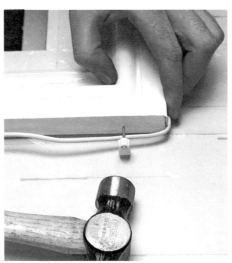

5 *Use cable clips round door and window frames to keep wiring out of sight. The wire itself is thin enough not to be prominent*

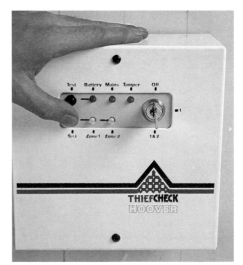

6 *Check the circuits according to the maker's instructions. This may involve nothing more than pressing the control unit 'Test' button*

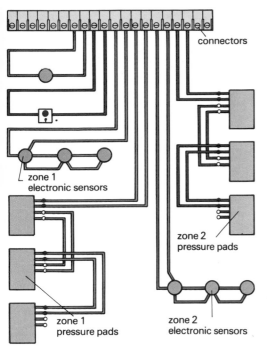

A typical wiring diagram for a 2-zone system, all the wires coming from the control unit. Exact details will vary from system to system so check the manufacturer's instructions before you start work

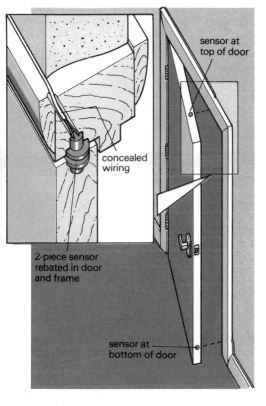

Locations for magnetic sensors in a door or window. They must be inconspicuous, with a gap between the components of less than 6mm

★ WATCH POINT ★

Check each stage of the wiring for continuity—in other words that a circuit has been made. This can generally be carried out at the control panel by operating the zone or selector switch governing the particular circuit. This will simplify any fault-finding that might be needed when the installation is complete.

These are ideal for use where drilling into the door or window frames is not possible—if you have metal frames for example. Consult the manufacturer before you buy.

7 Using an appropriate wood bit, drill into the edge of the door or window and into the frame immediately adjacent to it

8 Drill through the back of the door or window frame into the large hole. Use a drill just thicker than the wire you are installing

Fitting the pressure pads

A pressure pad is sensitive to weight and will actuate even through the thickness of a carpet when someone is standing on it. Beware though, that the weight of a dog—or even a cat—could cause the pad to operate and sound the alarm.

Ideal locations for a pressure pad are at the threshold of a door, on stair treads and beneath windows. If necessary, a pressure pad can be located directly in front of a particularly valuable item such as a wall safe or free-standing security cabinet.

Place pads directly on the floor and not between underlay and carpet. The surface of the floor must be clean and free from grit or abrasions.

Secure the pads using either adhesive tape or tacks pushed through the fixing tabs on the outside of the pad.

Connect the pads to the control box as instructed in the maker's handbook and test the circuit to ensure that it is operating satisfactorily.

★ WATCH POINT ★

A personal attack button will operate the alarm whether or not the control unit is switched on. Fitted in a bedroom or close to an exit this 'panic button' will help you to summon help if necessary. Be careful not to locate the button where young children might activate it.

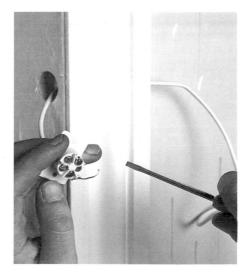

9 Feed the cable through the back of the frame and bare the ends before connecting the sensors according to the instructions

10 *If the carpet has an underlay, cut out a pad-shaped section so that the pressure pad lies flush and doesn't create a visible hump*

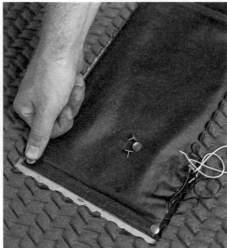

11 *Tape or pin the pressure pads in place, taking care not to pin through the sensor elements near the edges of the pad*

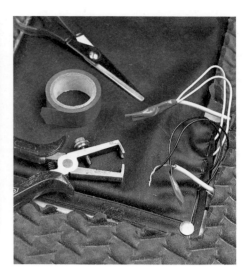

12 *Try if you can to run the wiring under the underlay, then tape the connections to the pad following the wiring diagram supplied*

Testing and commissioning

Before fully testing the complete alarm system, follow the maker's instructions for installing any necessary batteries.

You might need assistance to operate pressure pads and magnetic sensors and make sure that all components are properly secured.

Close all doors and windows fitted with sensors and reset personal attack buttons and remove activating keys.

Check, by pressing zone testing buttons, that all the systems are clear.

Now test each pad and sensor by opening doors and windows and applying weight to the pads. If you keep the appropriate zone test button depressed, activation will be indicated by the test light going out.

Repeat the test for all zones by following the maker's setting-up instructions.

A final tip: in case you lose the control keys, leave a spare with a trusted neighbour, or try to get a replacement key cut.

Living with an alarm

Pressure pads can become a nuisance if some form of discipline is not imposed on your family: it is all too easy to forget the alarm is switched on, especially during the day. Your first task must be to educate the family—especially younger members—to check the alarm is not switched on when they are moving around. A common mistake is to lay pressure pads under the carpet near an upstairs WC.

Remember also that the police don't take kindly to false alarms, however much they approve of home owners fitting burglar alarms. And there is nothing more infuriating to your neighbours than an alarm which comes on while you are away, but cannot be switched off.

If several of your neighbours have alarm systems fitted, it is worth setting up a 'self-help' group: if one of the alarms goes off, arrange between yourselves for someone to call the police to investigate. Quite apart from the security implications, it improves relations between yourselves. Relations will be improved even more if neighbours leave front door keys and alarm keys with trusted friends nearby so that an alarm which goes off accidentally can be switched off.

Prevention, as the police will always tell you, is better than cure. In fitting a burglar alarm system and using it properly, you are doing yourself a favour while at the same time making the police's job of crime prevention much easier.

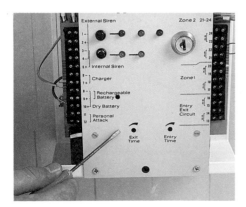

The entry/exit circuit timer may be adjustable using a screw in the control unit

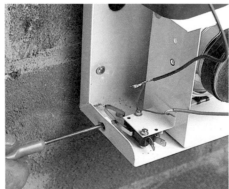

The anti-tamper devices should be tested before commissioning: use the manufacturer's guide

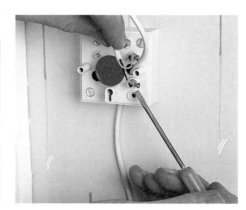

The personal attack button, or 'panic button', can be fitted much like a light switch

FIT A DOOR BELL

As you may know to your cost, the sound produced by a door knocker does not always carry well inside, particularly if the internal doors are closed and the TV is on: what you need is a far more versatile announcing system—an electric door bell.

The great advantage of an electric bell is that you can site it where it can be most easily heard. You can fit an extension bell to make the system more audible, and have bell pushes for both front and back doors.

Types of bells: Electric bells operate off very low voltages and the simplest types are battery powered (see Battery-powered bells). They're available individually or in kits, complete with a length of special thin two-core (twin) bell wire to connect to the power source, a bell push and all the fixings. You should be able to install a simple battery-powered bell system in about half an hour.

Door bells can also be powered from the mains, but you must fit a suitable transformer to reduce the mains voltage. If you decide on this system, you'll find there's a wider range of bells to choose from, but the initial costs are inevitably higher: a bell transformer can cost more than the bell kit itself. Installation will also take longer, because you have to make a connection into the mains supply.

Both battery and mains-powered electric bells are cheap to run. Batteries last about two years while a mains-powered bell will have little effect on your electricity bill.

Buying a bell

When you go to buy a bell, visit a store with several different types on 'live' display so that you can try them out and buy the one that suits you best. Bells, buzzers and chimes are all available while the more complex types can play a short peal and some models containing a cassette or programmed microprocessor can play a short tune.

If you want to fit two bell pushes, it's worth considering a unit which gives one signal for the front door and a slightly different one for the back.

A simple chime unit consists of an electromagnet wound round a sliding bar; at each end there's a striking plate or tube—these often hang down below the housing. When the bell push is depressed,

the bar is drawn through the electromagnet coil to strike one of the tubes. It's held in this position until the bell push is released when a spring throws the bar back through the coil to hit the chime tube on the other side—hence the familiar 'ding-dong'. Some models also incorporate a 'repeater' mechanism for keeping this action going as long as the bell push is depressed.

Probably the most familiar of door bells is the 'trembler' bell, so called because the sound it makes is created by a hammer vibrating furiously against a metal gong. The bell will continue to ring as long as the bell push is kept down.

With trembler bells, an electromagnet is again used to activate the striking arm, but as the arm moves 'make-and-break' contacts are opened, so closing the circuit. The arm returns to its starting position once it has struck the gong. Because the make-and-break contacts are now closed, the circuit is remade so the process repeats itself—at many times a second—until the circuit is finally broken when the bell push is released; the volume of the bell can be adjusted via a screw on the make-and-break contacts.

Trembler bells can operate off the direct current (DC) of batteries or the alternating current (AC) of the mains via a transformer. But you can also buy mains-operated trembler bells, which harness the alternating nature of the current to cause

the hammer to vibrate against the gong. These bells don't require make-and-break contacts so they're much easier to maintain.

If you aren't keen on a piercing ringing bell, then you can opt for a buzzer instead. This works in a similar way to the trembler bell, but the sound is made by a metal bar striking the electromagnet itself, rather than a gong. Again, battery and mains types are made.

Bell pushes

To operate any door bell you need a basic switching mechanism and this, simply, is what a bell push is. When you push the button you complete the circuit made with the bell wire; when you remove your finger a spring pushes the contacts apart.

The most basic types consist of a plastic base plate on which the switch mechanism is mounted; this is protected by a push-on cover, which also conceals the fixing screws. You can also buy brass and other ornate bell pushes to match your door furniture: they work in exactly the same way as the basic type. Some of the more elaborate pushes include a light, which illuminates the button or a name tag; useful features on a poorly lit doorstep. Because the light will stay on continuously illuminated pushes should only be used when the bell is run off the mains; a battery would run flat within two or three days. The miniature bulb inside may require occasional replacement.

Choosing a transformer

It's safest and easiest to buy a purpose-made transformer for your bell. These units normally contain a 1 amp fuse. The instructions with the bell will tell you what voltage it should be run on—commonly 3, 5 or 8 volts—and you'll find that most bell transformers have output (Secondary) terminals to match. Chimes usually have to be connected to the 8 volts terminals; bells and buzzers to the 5 or 3 volt terminals. You can also get transformers which supply higher voltages—commonly 4, 8 and 12 volts.

Siting the housing

Obviously, the bell push will have to be sited right by the door. The best place to site the bell housing is often in the hall where it can probably be heard throughout the house. An extension bell can be installed in a garage or shed, and if someone is hard of hearing then it's also worth putting another bell in the living-room, kitchen or other room that's used frequently.

Mount the bell high up on the wall so that it's inconspicuous and can't be knocked accidentally. This is particularly important for chimes with striking tubes that protrude down from the housing. Once you've determined the site, you can work out how you're going to run the bell wire to the bell push, and to the transformer. Fortunately, because bell wire is very thin its easy to conceal behind picture rails, skirting boards and architraves.

Obtaining power

There are basically four ways to connect your transformer. The simplest is to plug it into a three-pin socket outlet, replacing the plug's 13 amp fuse with a 3 amp one instead. But to avoid an unsightly run of flex, the transformer should be fitted next to the socket and this leaves it vulnerable to knocks. In addition, hallways, where bells are usually installed, tend to be short of sockets and you may have to unplug the transformer each time you want to operate your vacuum cleaner for example. To get around this, you could install a switched

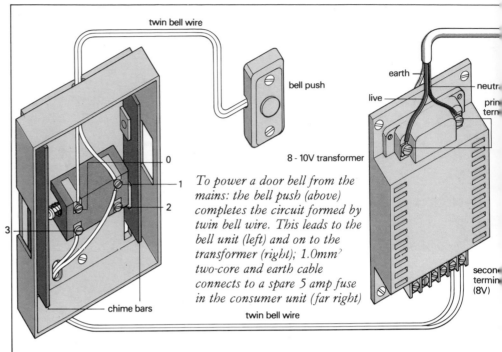

To power a door bell from the mains: the bell push (above) completes the circuit formed by twin bell wire. This leads to the bell unit (left) and on to the transformer (right); 1.0mm² two-core and earth cable connects to a spare 5 amp fuse in the consumer unit (far right)

fused connection unit, fitted with a 3 amp fuse, specifically for the transformer. This unit should be connected to a spur run in 2.5m² two-core and earth cable from the main power circuit; then 1.00mm² two-core and earth cable should be run to the primary terminals of the transformer itself. For full details on how to install a fused connection unit, see Add an extra socket, pages 74–77.

Similarly, you could break into the lighting circuit either by linking into a loop-in ceiling rose or by running a branch from a new three-terminal joint box installed on the supply cable. Unfortunately, to carry out the wiring you'll have to raise a few floorboards.

However, this does allow you to mount the transformer neatly by the side of the bell housing, especially if it's set high up on the wall. But as you're likely to be installing the bell close to the consumer unit—usually in the hallway—it makes sense to make your mains connection here.

If your consumer unit has a spare fuseway or spare miniature circuit breaker (MCB) the best way to obtain power for the transformer is to connect it to its own circuit protected by a 5 amp fuse or MCB.

Safety first

Electricity is potentially lethal if you don't treat it properly. So long as you make sure that the current is switched off before you touch any electrical fitting you cannot

possibly get a shock. But, although turning off the main switch will render the live parts dead, in some consumer units the mains terminals to which the meter leads connect aren't recessed, and there's still a risk of you receiving a shock. To be safe, it's wise to ask the electricity board to cut off the mains supply before you carry out any work on the consumer unit. When they restore the power they can also test your new circuit.

Installing a bell push and housing

When it comes to fitting a mains-powered door bell, all the work entails is installing a simple electric circuit. This consists of the bell push to activate the circuit, the wire to carry the current to the bell itself—and a transformer to provide the correct voltage.

Start by fitting the bell push. This is normally sited on the door frame at about chest height. It should be conspicuous, yet protected from the weather.

Hold the backplate of the unit to the frame and mark the position of the fixing holes and the bell wire entry using a

---

★ WATCH POINT ★

Bed the bell push on non-setting mastic if there's a danger that it might be exposed to rain.

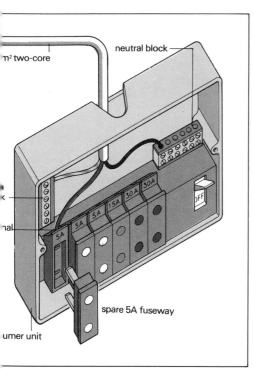

neutral block

m² two-core

spare 5A fuseway

umer unit

bradawl. Then drill a 6mm diameter hole through the frame so the bell wire can be fed into the back of the push. Screw the backplate in place using woodscrews—they're usually provided—and thread the bell wire through the hole in the door frame.

Separate the two insulated wire cores enough to allow them to reach the terminals on the backplate. Strip about 6mm of insulation from each of the cores and connect them to the terminals (it doesn't matter which way round they go), using a small electrician's screwdriver. Now draw any extra bell wire back through the hole—avoid straining the connections —and then clip on the bell push cover.

Next run the bell wire back to the site of the bell housing choosing the most inconspicuous route, usually along skirting and picture rails and around door frames. If

the bell wire is kinked, running it quickly through your hands a few times will warm and smooth it.

Keep the wire in place at 600mm intervals either with bell wire tacks, which you tap between the insulated cores, or with small cable clips that lap over both cores. You can also buy bell wire with a sticky strip on one side that you just press down to hold in place.

Remove the decorative cover from the bell housing and hold the backplate, which contains the bell mechanism, against the wall. Mark the fixing holes using a bradawl then drill and plug them. Run the bell wire from the push to the housing. Separate and strip back the insulation of the cores then connect them to the relevant terminals.

Fix the backplate, and connect to the transformer, then replace the cover.

Installing a bell transformer

The transformer reduces the mains voltage to the low level required for a doorbell. There are various ways to connect it—from simply plugging it into the mains at a three-pin socket to providing its own circuit from the consumer unit.

A bell transformer has two sets of terminals. At the top of the box the 'primary' terminals take the cable linking into the 240V mains supply; at the bottom the 'secondary' terminals take the twin bell wire from the bell housing. Make the connections by attaching the exposed bell wire cores to the correctly-rated screw-down terminals.

To connect into a spare fuseway in the consumer unit, first turn off the main switch (or have the mains supply cut off temporarily); remove the consumer unit cover and check that there's a spare (unconnected) fuseway the correct rating

for the transformer: 5 amp.

Once you have the correctly-rated fuseway installed, mount the transformer next to the consumer unit.

Attach a length of twin bell wire to the secondary terminals of the transformer and run it to the bell housing. Make the connections and attach the decorative cover.

> ★ WATCH POINT ★

If there's not a spare fuseway, you'll have to unscrew the live busbar and slide the existing fuseways along the busbar to make room for a new one. The fuseways must be arranged in the correct current rating sequence: highest (45 amp) next to the main switch; the lowest (5 amp) at the opposite end.

Strip and connect the live (red) and the neutral (black) cores of a length of 1.0mm² two-core and earth cable to the primary terminals of the transformer. If the transformer doesn't need to be earthed, then ignore the earth core and tape it back out of the way.

Run the cable to the entry point of the consumer unit, fastening it down with cable clips. Remove enough of the cable's outer

> ★ WATCH POINT ★

It's best to make all the connections—from the push to the bell housing and on to the transformer—before you make the mains connections. This lessens the time you'll have to have the power switched off.

1 *To fit the push, drill through the door frame from both sides using tape guide*

2 *Feed a length of twin bell wire through the door frame and connect up the bell push*

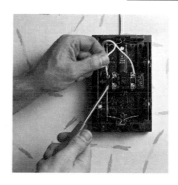

3 *Slot the bell wire into the housing, screw the unit to wall and connect the terminals*

4 *Run in more bell wire from the housing to transformer and make the connections*

sleeve so there's about 25mm remaining inside the box. Strip off about 10mm of insulation from each core. Connect the live core to the terminal at the top of the spare fuseway and take the neutral core to the neutral block. Link the earth core (which must be sleeved in green/yellow PVC) to the earth terminal.

Have the supply restored and turn on the main switch. Test the bell to ensure that everything works properly.

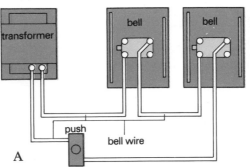

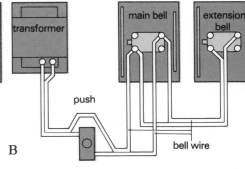

A

B

Alternative ideas

You might not be able to hear the front doorbell from certain parts of the house—especially if the internal doors are shut, or you're in the garden. The answer here is to fit an extension bell.

You can either wire the two bells in 'series' or in 'parallel' (see diagrams). The advantage of the first method is that the two bells are connected in the same circuit, so one bell won't rob the other of power. You'll need to reconnect the bell wire in the transformer to higher voltage terminals.

To wire two bells in series:
• connect the push to the transformer with a single core of bell wire
• connect the push to one bell with a single core of bell wire
• join the two bells with another single core
• run a single core from the second bell to the transformer.

The advantages of bells wired in parallel is that if one breaks down the other will still work. Both bells must be of the same type and while strictly you don't have to double the operating voltage, it is advisable to do so.

To wire two bells in parallel:
• connect twin bell wire to the transformer
• split one core and connect up the push
• run the twin bell wire on to the first bell

Wire an extension bell: in series (A)—both bells in the same circuit so one won't rob the other of power; or in parallel (B)—if one should fail the other will still function

• run a further length of twin bell wire on to the second bell and make the connections.

Battery-powered bells

If you don't want to go to the trouble and expense of fitting a transformer, a battery-operated door bell is the answer. With most chimes and some bells, the batteries fit inside the unit.

Rather than using one large battery, usually two or four 1½V 'baby' or 'mono' batteries are used instead. These are arranged in series to give the required voltage. They're slotted into place against spring terminals, and the direction in which they should be set is clearly marked with arrows and positive and negative symbols. The doorbell won't function unless the batteries are the right way round.

Many bells and most buzzers don't make provision for the batteries to be housed internally. Instead they run off a larger battery (usually 4½V) which have to be mounted nearby.

To wire up a bell to a battery, connect a

length of twin bell wire to the terminals inside the bell or buzzer unit. Run one core to the bell push and then link a separate single core from the push to the negative ( ) terminal of the battery. The two cores of the bell wire are easy to separate simply by pulling them apart. Next run a single core of bell wire from the positive (+) terminal of the battery to connect up the free end of the bell wire from the bell housing.

You can't connect two trembler bells together if the circuit is run off batteries: the first bell would prevent the second one from operating properly. To get round this problem either fit an AC powered bell or join the make-and-break contacts of the second bell with a core of bell wire.

You'll need twice the voltage to power an extension bell. Either fit a more powerful battery or connect two 4½V batteries in series (negative to positive) with bell wire.

★ WATCH POINT ★

High power (HP) batteries last longer than ordinary ones: make sure you use the sealed type. When the batteries run down, change them immediately—don't leave them in the unit, where they may corrode.

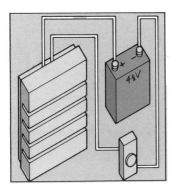

A battery circuit consists of battery, push and bell connected with twin bell wire

To power an extension bell you'll need two 4½V batteries wired in series

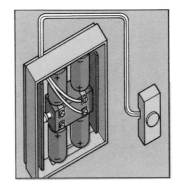

Four 1½V batteries will power a single bell, and can be fitted inside the unit

Bell wire cores are easy to separate: nick the sheathing then pull apart the cores

DOOR ANSWERING SYSTEM

Door answering systems are generally found in blocks of flats, where the occupants can identify and admit callers without having to descend several flights of stairs to the door. But such a system can also be equally suited to any home: it's an excellent complement to a burglar alarm, stout door and window locks and any other home security devices.

A typical system

A door answering system is a simple intercom facility. It basically comprises a telephone-style handset, which is mounted in the house where it can most conveniently be answered—the kitchen, for instance, or hallway, study or living room.

Multi-core flex runs from the handset to a push-button external unit, which you fix onto the wall outside by the front door (or with some units, actually set within the door). The external unit contains a microphone, a receiving amplifier and a speaker (which may have volume control).

When a caller presses a button on the external unit, a buzzer sounds on the handset. By lifting the telephone receiver, the occupant opens a channel to the speaker and receiver. The occupant can then enquire who is there and also hear the caller's reply.

The system operates on low voltage, provided via a transformer, which you must mount out of harm's way (next to the consumer unit is both safe and convenient). The transformer can be connected to the mains by wiring it into a spare 5 amp fuseway although it is possible to run it off a spur fused connection unit, wire it into the lighting circuit or simply plug it into an ordinary socket outlet.

Siting the system

Exactly where you site the system depends on the layout of your house. Aim to site the handset where it can most conveniently be reached.

The external unit can be positioned directly outside your front door or, if you live in a house with a long driveway surrounded by a wall or fence, the unit can be fitted on the gate or doorway at the boundary.

The flex connecting the unit and handset can be run inconspicuously along the inside walls in plastic conduit, or with more trouble be neatly located in channels cut in the wall.

If the cable is to run to a gate outside, bury it in a trench dug in the ground for neatness. This also prevents accidental damage from garden tools, although as the answering system runs on low voltage, there's no danger of receiving a dangerous electric shock.

Tools and materials

To install a door answering system the only materials you need, apart from the kit, are: a quantity of multi-core telephone cable to reach from the outside panel to the handset and transformer; a length of 1.0mm^2 two-core and earth PVC-sheathed cable if you plan to connect to the mains; and if necessary, a fused connection unit to tee into the ring main.

You'll need few tools to install the unit: a tape measure, marking knife, chisel, mallet, screwdriver, and an electric drill with wood and masonry bits (bit size depends on the kit so consult the manufacturer's instructions) is ample for fixing the panels to the wall and drilling the cable holes in the front door frames, if necessary.

Secure the multi-core cable runs in place or you may find yourself tripping over them. Ordinary telephone cable securing clips will do.

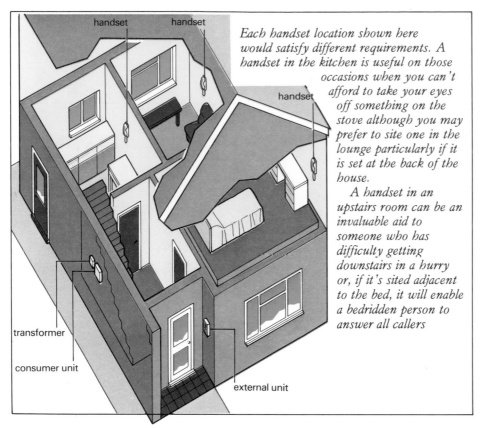

handset   handset

handset

transformer

consumer unit

external unit

Each handset location shown here would satisfy different requirements. A handset in the kitchen is useful on those occasions when you can't afford to take your eyes off something on the stove although you may prefer to site one in the lounge particularly if it is set at the back of the house.

A handset in an upstairs room can be an invaluable aid to someone who has difficulty getting downstairs in a hurry or, if it's sited adjacent to the bed, it will enable a bedridden person to answer all callers

Fitting the door panel and handset

The first job is to position the external unit and the handset. There are basically two ways you can fit the external unit: by surface-mounting it, or recessing it in the wall for neatness. The handset is simply surface-mounted inside the house.

For comfortable use, the external unit should be positioned about 1.4m above the ground, so that callers will be able to introduce themselves and receive your reply without having to stoop unduly. If you can, position the unit in a sheltered location so that visitors receive some protection from the rain during wet weather.

If you're surface-mounting the external unit on the wall by your front door, you can simply screw it into pre-drilled and plugged holes. Remove the cover from the unit and hold the base box against the wall in the required position.

Mark through the fixing holes with a pencil (or bradawl if the holes are too small). Remove the box and drill holes at the marked positions. Insert wall plugs then return the box to the wall and screw it into place.

★ WATCH POINT ★

Surface-mounted panels usually have plastic cases that are water resistant, but you should, where possible, site the unit where it won't be exposed to driving rain. You may think it worthwhile constructing a wooden box around the panel as extra protection.

Answering systems intended for flush-mounting have metal—not plastic—base boxes like those used for conventional mains electrical appliances, incorporating knock-outs for cable entry and fitted with lugs for fixing to the wall. The knock-outs may be situated all round the base box to give you plenty of choice when running the cable. Only punch one out when you've decided.

To fit a flush-mount box, hold the box, faceplate removed, against the wall and draw round it in chalk. Try to position the

1 *Position the external unit about 1.4m above the ground. Mark the wall, through the fixing holes, with a bradawl making sure the unit is straight*

2 *At each mark, drill out a hole using a masonry bit. Plug the holes and then secure the external unit with the screws provided*

3 *Screw the handset's backplate to a wall at a chosen location inside the house. Prepare the wires ready for connection*

unit so that you will not have to cut too many bricks; position it between horizontal courses, too, for this reason.

Chop out a hole in the wall using a club hammer and bolster chisel. Keep the sides of the hole as smooth as possible to save unnecessary making good later. Don't cut too deeply, either: you need only go as deep as the box itself, and this is likely to be approximately 75mm.

Clean up the inside of the hole and try the base box for fit: if it fits well, simply mark the wall through the screw holes, drill and insert wallplugs, and then screw the box to the masonry.

Don't forget to knock out the blank circle in the metal box to accommodate the cable at the point of entry. At this stage you can leave the unit without mortaring it in place, in case any adjustments need to be made at a later stage.

The next job is to fit the handset to the wall inside the house. Aim to fix it about 1.5m above the floor for convenient use. Remove the cover then hold the backplate against the wall. Mark the fixing holes, drill and insert wallplugs, then screw the unit to the wall.

Now position the transformer between handset and the external unit. The two units are now ready for connecting up. However, if your set includes an automatic door latch this must be fitted first. Remove the old latch before you start.

Fitting a remote control door latch

You can fit an automatic door latch, which can be operated by depressing a button on the system's handset. Latches can be either set on the architrave or recessed into the door frame, depending on the type of lock in use—check when you buy.

Basically, most door answering systems are designed to work with rim locks. There are mortise lock versions but they are rarely used in ordinary domestic installations. With both types, when the button on the handset is depressed, the latch is electrically activated and the door can then be pushed open by the caller in order to enter.

Whichever type you're fitting, first hold it in position against the door frame and draw around it in pencil, to indicate where you'll have to cut the frame.

For a rim latch type, use a bevel-edged chisel to chop a recess for the device; for a mortise latch type (should you happen to have obtained one of these) you'll have to drill a series of holes within the marked out

4 *If you're fitting an automatic door latch, your first job must be to remove the old latch from the door frame*

mortise, then use a chisel to remove the waste, forming a square-sided slot. Fix the device in its recess with the screws provided.

The cable to the mortise type of automatic latch enters the device from the rear, so you'll have to drill a small hole through the door frame to slot it in. Feed the end of a length of multi-core cable into the hole and connect two of the cores to the terminals on the latch. Slide the latch into position and make sure you secure it firmly.

With the mechanism fixed to the frame, close the door and mark the position of the keep plate or the bolt box. Screw the keep plate inside the face of the door or cut a recess for the bolt box on the more rarely used mortise type latch.

Manually test the operation of the latch to make sure the action is smooth and make any necessary adjustments.

Making the electrical connections

You can power your door answering system by simply plugging the transformer into a spare 13 amp socket outlet. Alternatively, run a spur from the lighting circuit or a branch from the ring main. By far the best arrangement however, is to site the transformer next to the consumer unit and simply run a length of 1.0mm² two-core and earth cable from it to a spare 5 amp (lighting) fuse. With a double insulated transformer, you won't need to use the earth core so just cut it right back out of the way.

If you just want to run the door

5 *Hold the new latch over the old recess and mark it with a pencil. Enlarge the rebate with a bevel-edged chisel*

6 *Check that the lock on the door engages cleanly with the latch before tightening up the securing screws*

answering system transformer from an existing socket outlet, connect the live (brown) and neutral (blue) cores of a length of 1.0mm² two-core flex to the relevant terminals of the transformer—following the manufacturer's instructions fully—and wire up the other end to a three-pin plug, then make the connections from transformer to door answering system as described later on.

To run a branch from the ring circuit, first switch off at the mains, or remove the relevant fuse. You'll need to fit a fused connection unit between the mains supply and the transformer (see page 52). Break into the ring circuit at the nearest available power socket. Most transformers don't

7 *Connect the wires from the unit and telephone to the remotely-controlled latch. Strip back the wires and connect according to instructions*

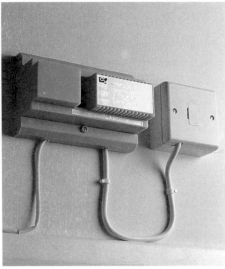

8 *There are several ways of connecting the transformer to the mains. One method is to run a fused spur from the ring main*

relevant terminals in the handset. Run the cable to the external unit and connect the cores to the terminals there. Run another length of flex from the handset to the transformer, this time connecting only the blue core and taping back the others.

Connect the blue, green and pink cores of another length of cable between the transformer and external unit. Finally, run another length of cable between transformer and external unit, connecting only the blue core to the terminals indicated in the kit instructions.

Although this method involves quite a few separate runs of cable, it's preferable to the alternative's splitting the individual cores with additional lengths of bell wire.

When you're satisfied that the connections are good, replace the terminal cover on the transformer, then secure the runs of cable between units using small cable clips or, for neatness, insert them in plastic conduit. If you've chased out the wall, fit in

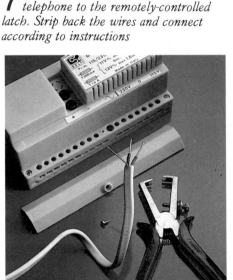

9 *Use 1.0mm² twin core and earth cable to connect the transformer to the mains*

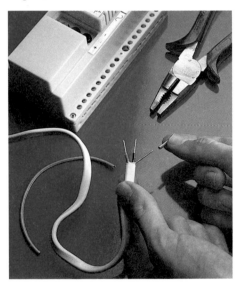

10 *If you need to use the earth core, sheath the exposed core with green and yellow sleeving*

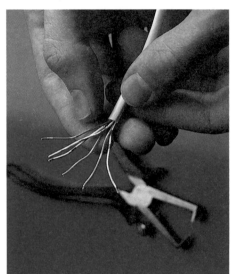

11 *The wires in telephone cable are not very robust so take care when you prepare the cores*

need to be earthed, so you can just ignore the earth core.

Alternatively, you can connect the cable into an existing loop-in ceiling rose and run it to the transformer.

For more details on identifying ring main circuits, loop-in ceiling roses and installing junction boxes, see pages 49–52 and 19–22.

The connections to the door answering system's handset and the external unit are made with multi-core telephone cable. This typically has blue, red, orange, yellow, green, pink, black and white cores but as the core colours vary so much it's difficult to

give categoric guidance. The best thing to do is study the diagram opposite, note which wires lead where and then run your own wires to match those routes exchanging the colours used in the diagram for the core colours in the cable you are using.

First run a cable between the automatic door latch and the transformer: only two cores are necessary here, so cut back the others. Insert the cores in the terminals.

Now connect the red, orange and yellow cores (or whatever colours you've chosen from those on your cable to fulfil this purpose) of another length of cable to the

the cable and make good the channels with plaster.

Switch on the power at the mains (or replace the circuit fuse) then test the system.

Reinforcing the door

Although an automatic door latch offers a degree of security, it means you won't be able to fit other locks, except for night-latches. In this case it's worth reinforcing the door frame.

At its simplest, reinforcement can mean

fitting good quality hinge bolts, which won't strengthen the opening side of the door but will ward against forced entry from the hinge side.

To fit the bolts, first mark the position of the bolt on the hinge edge of the door and drill a hole—likely to be about 10mm diameter and 38mm deep—to take the ribbed part of the bolt.

Hammer in the ribbed end of the bolt then partially close the door so the bolt will mark the jamb. At this point drill a 12mm diameter hole for the depth of the bolt, mark up for the mating metal plate, then chisel a recess in the jamb for it.

Screw the plate into position then test the operation of the door to make sure it doesn't bind.

There are various proprietary devices available for strengthening the door without hindering its action: anti-jemmy plates are small metal strips which you can hammer

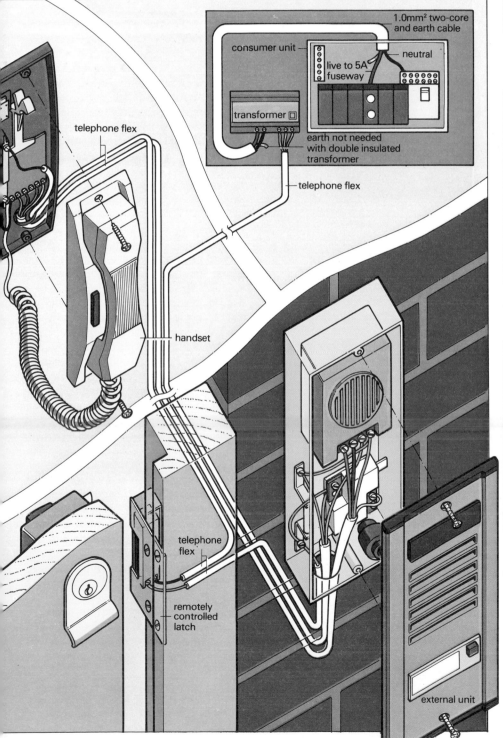

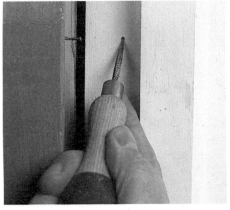

Tap a nail into the door's edge—it will leave a mark opposite on the frame

Drill out a hole in the door and hammer in the ribbed end of the bolt

Chisel a recess in the frame to take the plate and drill another hole for the bolt

into the door jamb to deter thieves from using a jemmy or crowbar to force open the door.

Reinforcing strips, which you fit around the door frame, are also a good method of protecting the door frame from forcing. Simply measure around the frame, order the relevant amount of strip and screw it to the timber, as described in the manufacturer's instructions.

CENTRAL HEATING CONTROLS

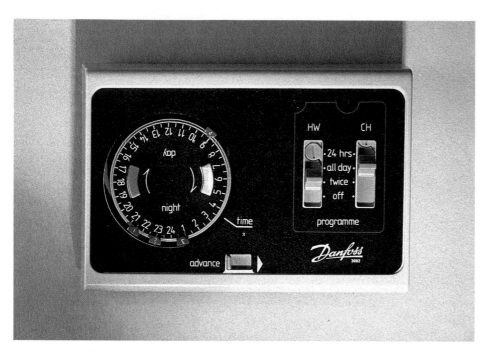

Central heating systems, even new ones, tend to be fitted with the bare minimum of controls. This means that they are often running inefficiently, either by giving out heat where it isn't needed, or by not heating rooms adequately. By adding supplementary controls to the system, it is possible to obtain a more balanced performance and make substantial savings in running costs into the bargain.

How this is achieved depends upon the individual design of the system and the type of controls already in use. To see where your system is lacking, compare it with the schematic diagram of an ideal fully automated system opposite.

None of the schemes mentioned below, however, is suitable for solid fuel boilers. Also, low water content gas boilers with copper heat exchangers may require a bypass valve to prevent a build-up of heat when the controls are off. Any boiler manufacturer's recommendations on how you adapt your system must take precedence over the advice given here.

Areas to consider

Work your way through your existing system, looking at its functions and making a note of any obvious deficiencies.

The boiler: Both gas and oil boilers are now controlled by an integral electrical thermostat. This keeps the water inside the heat exchanger at a constant temperature—igniting the burners as the temperature falls and extinguishing the flame as the temperature is restored.

Domestic hot water: On conventional systems, the domestic hot water is stored in a cylinder. The control of the water temperature is primarily through the boiler thermostat. On the crudest gravity systems, this is the sole means of controlling the water temperature at the taps. This has two major disadvantages.

When the central heating is turned on, the water in the cylinder is automatically heated to the same temperature as the water in the radiators. There are many occasions when you need a different temperature in each individual circuit.

When the heating is turned off, the boiler will remain hot all the time the domestic hot water circuit is switched on. This means that although the cylinder may be full of hot water the boiler will be switching on and off under the instruction of its own thermostat merely to keep the water in the boiler hot. Because the boiler is not insulated this cycling effect will continue every few

minutes as heat is lost through the flue and through the casing.

What is needed is a means of telling the boiler that the cylinder is hot enough. An electrical cylinder thermostat is designed to do this by sensing the temperature of the water in the cylinder and sending a signal to shut off the boiler.

This is a perfectly adequate arrangement as long as the hot water only is required. But as soon as the radiator circuits are brought into use the water temperature in the cylinder is once again governed by the boiler thermostat. To overcome this a valve (mechanical or electro-mechanical) is needed to shut off the water returning from the cylinder circuit, thus giving independent temperatures in the radiators and at the taps.

The programmer: Central heating programmers are designed to control all the different components of a central heating system, giving an automatic switching operation through the timeclock.

The radiators: The majority of radiator circuits are assisted by an electrical pump which greatly accelerates the speed of water passing through the system. Switching the pump on and off is the simplest method of controlling the room temperatures. Usually, a room thermostat mounted on the wall is used to control the pump. But inevitably this leads to a compromise.

The answer lies in local control. Depending on the layout of the pipework one of two methods may be adopted.

The most effective is to fit individual *thermostatic radiator valves* which control the temperature of each radiator.

The other method is control by *zone valves*. A fundamental requirement of this is that pipework must be easily divided into separate runs. A careful examinination of the system will determine the feasibility of this scheme.

Where the pipework branches to supply the upstairs and ground floor on two separate circuits, zone valves may be effectively employed to operate each circuit independently.

In some cases this cannot be done. Many systems installed in houses with solid ground floors drop individual radiator circuits from the first floor. Individual thermostatic radiator valves are the best bet if you have this type of system.

If it's decided that a zone valve is feasible, a means of switching it on and off will be required. A simple room thermostat located within the zone is probably the best method; alternatively a time clock may be used so the upstairs circuits are automatically switched off when the bedrooms are not in use.

Any plumbing work will entail draining the system—but don't do this before you have established which pipes are which. Often, this can only be done by feeling which pipes become hot and in what order. Electrical work is best tackled separately.

Tools for the job

Most systems can be worked on with relatively few tools. For plumbing work you will need a junior hacksaw, an adjustable spanner, a radiator valve key and something to raise floorboards—a brick bolster or crowbar, for example.

Electrical work requires a small screwdriver and a pair of pliers. You may need to use a battery and bell continuity tester to trace the more complicated circuits.

Fitting thermostatic radiator valves

When fitting thermostatic radiator valves to an existing system, it is essential to

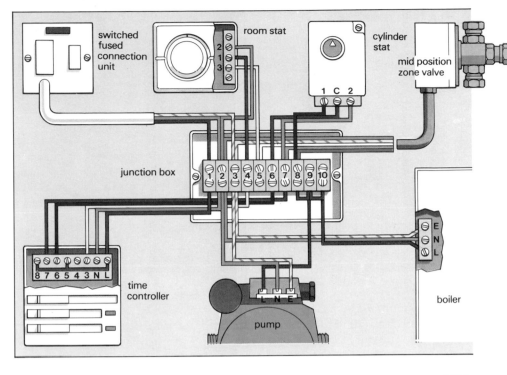

maintain an open circuit for the pump. This can be done by leaving one radiator with a manual valve always open or by fitting a bypass pipe between the flow and return on the heating side. The result of this is to stabilize the load on the pump, and it also helps to overcome noise problems.

Thermostatic radiator valves will only work if they are connected to the flow—you'll need to find the flow pipe on each radiator before you drain the system.

To find out which is the flow, turn the system off and allow it to cool, then turn it

The wiring circuit has heat-resistant PVC or butyl rubber cable within the boiler casing and standard 1.5mm² cable to link all the components to the junction box

back and feel both the pipes on each radiator. The flow pipe is the one which gets hot first—label it.

The system can now be drained by tying up the ball valve and opening the drain cock at the lowest point. Also open the air cocks on the radiators to allow water to drain down more easily.

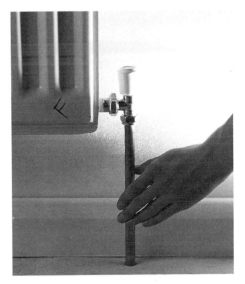

1 *Determine which pipe is the feed by turning the system off, letting it cool then turning it on and feeling which pipe heats up first*

2 *Remove the standard valve and copper pipe if it's too short; then wrap PTFE tape around the threads of the new valve body*

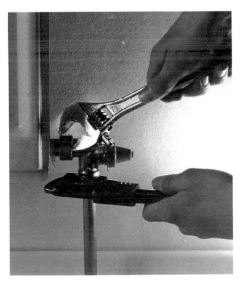

3 *Tighten the threaded connections, avoiding distortion to the pipework by holding the valve body firmly with a spanner*

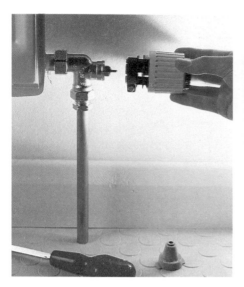

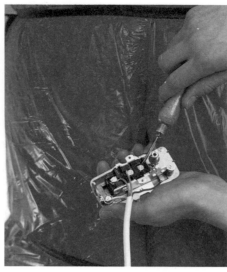

4 *Attach the actuator to the valve body, screwing the knurled nut finger-tight; then fill the system and check for leaks*

5 *Switch off the electricity and connect a three-core cable from the cylinder thermostat to the controller*

When the system is empty, hold the valve steady and undo the nuts on the pipework and radiator. You should then be able to slip off the old valve and place it on one side. Remove the threaded shank from the radiator using a radiator valve key.

The nut and olive on the pipe can be removed either by tapping the nut gently upwards until the olive is forced off or by carefully cutting through the olive with a junior hacksaw—be sure not to cut the pipe.

Offer up the new valve to the radiator and check that the copper pipe is long enough to locate correctly inside the valve body. If you find the pipe is too short there may be enough free play to draw it up a little. If not, the pipe will have to be cut further down and a new section joined in. The neatest way of doing this is to solder a new capillary connector on to the existing pipework.

The next step is to fix the new shank into the radiator. Wrap some PTFE tape around the threaded section and screw it into the radiator with a hexagonal radiator spanner. Fit the valves as shown, then fill the system once more and check for leaks.

Fitting an electrical cylinder thermostat

A cylinder thermostat does not require any plumbing work. The thermostat is held against the outside of the cylinder by means of a metal strap or curtain wire.

The position of the thermostat on the cylinder will determine the volume of water heated before the sensor operates. The usual position is somewhere around the

6 *Secure the thermostat to the hot water cylinder with the metal strap provided or a length of curtain wire*

middle of the lower half.

If the cylinder is factory-lagged with urethane foam, a cutout must be made with a sharp knife to expose a small section of the copper surface. Use the body of the thermostat as a template.

Run a three-core cable from the cylinder thermostat to the programmer and connect them up. Before removing the cover on the programmer, however, make sure that you switch off the electricity.

You will now have to find which wire goes from the programmer to the boiler. Many programmers have a small diagram to help identify the terminals. The terminal will be named 'hot water on'. Disconnect the live wire from this terminal and connect

the new wire from the cylinder thermostat terminal marked 'make on fall in temperature' or 'demand'.

Join the 'common' terminal on the cylinder thermostat to the live supply for the boiler.

The remaining terminal on the cylinder thermostat marked 'make on rise' must be connected to the central heating terminal that supplies power to the pump. It may be joined on the room thermostat terminal or anywhere between the room thermostat and the pump.

This will supply an alternative route to power the boiler when the cylinder thermostat is off and the heating is on.

Fitting a thermostatic cylinder valve

The ideal position for a cylinder valve is on the return pipe from the cylinder to the boiler. Often lack of space makes this impractical and another position must be sought. It is essential that the valve does not restrict the open vent or cold feed from the header tank. Note also that this valve is only for use on indirect systems.

You may need to reposition the cold feed to join the return pipe after the valve. You can do this fairly easily using compression fittings but you'll need to blank off the original cold feed pipe with a compression stop end.

The remote sensor must be placed against the copper of the cylinder and held firmly in position by the tape provided. The temperature adjustment is made by revolving the head of the valve, so this must be accessible.

Turn off the boiler and drain the system completely before commencing the installation. Offer up the valve and clearly mark two cutting lines on the pipe. Using a junior hacksaw, cut out the section between the lines and clean up the cut with a file.

Provided there is some free play in the pipework you should be able to slip in the valve and the compression joints.

If you find this impossible, disconnect the pipe at the cylinder union and reconnect

---

★ **WATCH POINT** ★

Incorporate an air cock into the blanking-off fitting so you will be able to bleed the system easily when you are refilling it.

7 *Gently uncoil the connecting pipe, place the remote capillary sensor against the cylinder and secure it with the tape provided*

thermostat is critical in obtaining an accurate sensing of the room temperature as a whole.

The most common position is either in the hall or the lounge. A case can be argued for either of these areas being better than the other, but really it is a matter of personal preference, since neither is perfect. In the end your decision may be influenced by which place offers the easiest route for running the cable, especially if you want to conceal it.

However, there are a number of positions that are *not* suitable. The unit must be kept clear of any heat source such as a radiator, a table or wall lamp, a television set or the direct rays of the sun. It must also be mounted away from draughts. The recommended height from the floor is 1500mm so when you have taken all these things into consideration your choice may be limited.

likely to leave home for more than a few days during the winter, a frost thermostat can be fitted to fire the boiler when temperatures fall to 5°C.

All that is required is a live supply run through the frost thermostat to the boiler and pump (see page 69).

Fitting a zone valve

Fitting a zone valve involves the same plumbing work as fitting a cylinder valve.

After draining the system, cut through the pipe with a junior hacksaw and secure the valve by means of the compression fittings. The system can be filled and tested

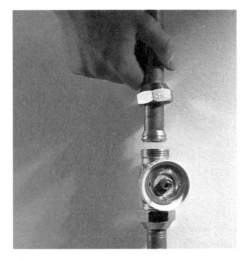

10 *Having drained the system, cut through the supply pipe at the appropriate point, insert the valve and tighten the fittings*

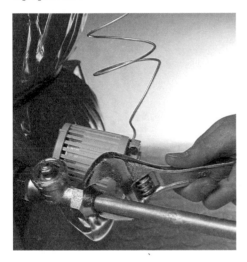

8 *Having drained the system, cut a section from the cold feed and insert the valve, tightening the fittings on either side*

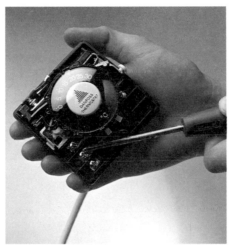

9 *Run a cable from the thermostat to the junction box and mount the unit in a hall or lounge away from any heat source*

when the valve is in place. Tighten the compression fitting on each side of the valve and fill the system with the valve fully open. Check the operation of the valve.

Fitting a wall-mounted thermostat

A wall-mounted thermostat can be used to control a pump, a diverter valve or a zone valve. The basic wiring principle is the same for all three in that the thermostat interrupts the electricity in exactly the same way as an ordinary light switch.

Because the switching action is activated by air temperature, the positioning of the

With the mains power off, connect the 'heating on' terminal at the programmer to the room thermostat 'common' terminal. The wire leaving the thermostat must be connected to the 'demand' or 'calling for heat' terminal. This will pass a live current to power the component.

Modern room thermostats incorporate a tiny heating element in the unit to improve the response of the heat sensor. The element requires a neutral connection, which can be taken from the programmer junction box.

Frost thermostat: A variation of a room thermostat is made to provide frost protection during very cold weather. If your boiler is located in an outhouse or you are

11 *Run a cable from the valve plug to the junction box; then simply connect the plug, fill the system and check for any leaks*

before commencing the electrical work.

If you're fitting a 22mm valve to old imperial ¾in. copper, change the olives in the fittings for ¾in. olives which are still available from good plumbers' merchants. You can fit a 22mm valve to 15mm pipe by inserting reducing sets into the ends of the fittings and tightening just like an ordinary joint.

Zone valves are available in two different types: spring return valves which require power only to open, and fully motorized valves requiring power to switch on and off.

Whether you intend to switch the valve by means of a thermostat, an ordinary light switch or directly from the programmer, the wiring is the same; all motorized valves require a neutral connection and an earth.

Some valves have an auxiliary wire to supply current to another component when the valve is fully open. This is useful in ensuring that the pump is open. It may also be used to power an indicator light.

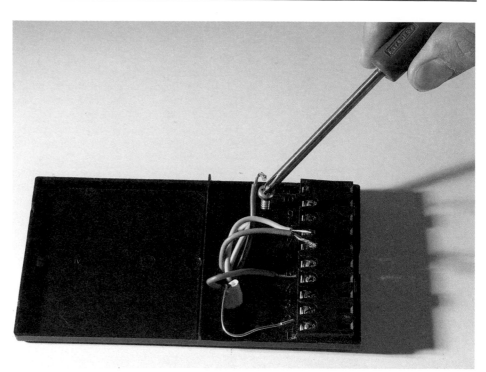

12 *Feed all the necessary wires through the backplate of the programmer and mount it on the wall in the most convenient position*

Fitting a new programmer

Modern programmers are made in two parts —the backplate, which screws on the wall and takes the wiring, and the control box which all the timing circuitry and clips on when the wiring is complete.

Cables can enter the box either through the back or the sides, giving you a choice of surface-run or concealed wiring.

The power supply for the programmer should be from a 3 amp fused connection unit or a plug and socket. Some programmers have a built-in junction box; others have a separate one.

All the neutrals and earths can be run directly from the junction box to the components. Switching is carried out on the live pole only (see page 69).

The terminals in the programmer are designated for switching power to the heating and hot water circuits. Where thermostats are fitted, the terminals will be connected to the thermostats first, and then on to any motorized valves and finally to the pump and central heating boiler.

When switching on for the first time, many solid state programmers have to charge their batteries before normal operation is achieved—so an initial lack of activity is not always an indication that you have put a wire in the wrong place.

Types of programmer. There are essentially two types of programmer: the analogue and the digital time switch.

The analogue type can be used to programme the on and off times of the central

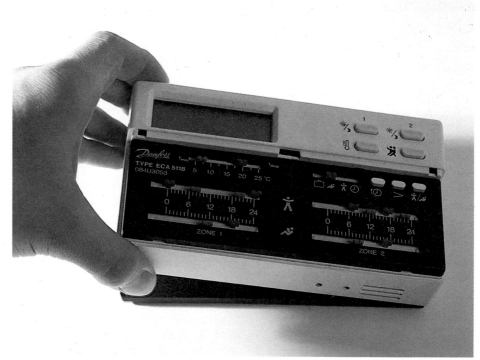

13 *Connect the wires to the appropriate terminals, then fit the control box to the backplate and then reconnect the power supply*

heating and domestic hot water systems independently. In addition, remote timer/night thermostats are available which can be used to maintain a temperature at night.

The more sophisticated digital types can display the temperatures both inside and outside the house and in different zones, and feature an override button for parties and late-night gatherings plus zone change-over buttons to swap the operation of the zone regulators.

CHAPTER 6

WIRING AND REWIRING

If your power points are in the wrong place, or your wiring is worn and dangerously outdated, now is the time to renew or extend your system. All the information you need is included, from adding an extra socket and providing an outside power supply to completely rewiring your home

ADD AN EXTRA SOCKET

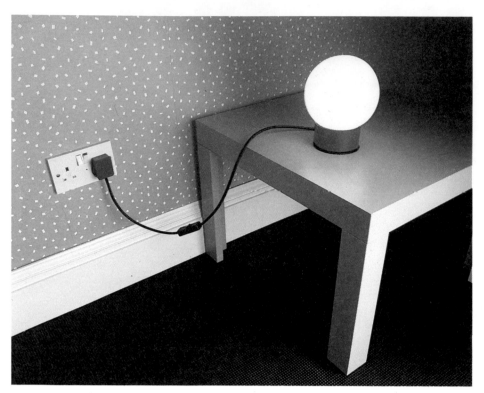

Where the power comes from

If you want to add a new socket outlet, the power does not have to come all the way from the consumer unit or fuse board—it can be drawn from any suitable existing outlet as long as you do not overload the circuit.

Start by determining whether you have a ring or a radial circuit. If you do not know already, switch off at the mains. Unscrew the faceplates of three sockets around the house. Pull each faceplate away from the wall and examine the wires carefully. Sockets wired on a ring main have two sets of cable, each consisting of a red live wire, a black neutral wire and a green/yellow earth. Those on a radial main have just one set of wires. You may be unlucky enough to choose a socket which is an 'extra socket' itself or is the power source for somewhere else. So continue opening up sockets until you have established a definite pattern.

Before you add an extra socket, make sure that you do not overload the circuit.

On a ring circuit you can safely add a socket provided that the existing circuit you intend to 'tap' does not exceed a floor area of 100 sq m—and that you do not go outside this area when you fit the new socket outlet.

On a radial circuit the floor area served

There are a number of different types of socket outlet so make sure that you choose the right one before you start. Flush-mounted outlets are the most common and obviously the neatest. They consist of a steel backing box recessed and fixed into the wall and a faceplate which screws on to the front.

Surface-mounted outlets are installed where it is difficult or impractical to cut a hole in an existing wall. They have a square backing box which is fixed directly to the wall and a faceplate—identical to the flush mounted plate—which is screwed on to the front. Most surface-mounted sockets are made of white plastic but you can also buy strong, impact-resistant metal boxes and faceplates for a garage or workshop.

Even if you fit a surface-mounted outlet you still have to hide the cable. The obvious way is to cut a channel for it through the wall. But you can avoid the bother that this entails by using *plastic conduit* or *mini-trunking*. Here the cable is led through a neat surface-mounted plastic channel which runs along the top of the skirting board or up the side of an architrave. Many conduit systems come complete with their own surface-mounted socket outlets as well as angled adapters which allow you to turn corners and right angles. Note, though, that

Trailing wires are messy and dangerous. Tidy them up by installing new sockets

existing flush outlets have to be converted to the surface mounted type if power is taken from them (see page 76).

Whatever type of socket you decide to fit remember that it is always possible to install a double rather than a single outlet—although you will need to cut out a larger recess to fit a flush-mounted socket.

Fused connection units

If you want to install an extra outlet in a bathroom—for a wall heater or towel rail, for instance—it would be dangerous (and in Britain against the electrical regulations) to use a plug and socket. Instead you must install a *fused connection unit*—a fitting which links the appliance directly and permanently to the power supply.

The unit is fitted and wired in a similar way to a socket outlet and can be either flush or surface mounted. A number of different faceplates are available—so examine the range carefully before you buy. For instance, some are switched and some have a pilot light which tells you when the unit is on or off.

★ WATCH POINT ★

Electricity is dangerous if you do not treat it properly. But as long as you make sure that the current is switched off before you touch any electrical fitting you cannot possibly get a shock.

Before you start work, switch off the house power supply with the main switch on the consumer unit or fuse board. A final check which will guarantee that any particular wire is disconnected is to use a mains tester screwdriver. This is an insulated screwdriver with a small neon bulb in the handle. If the blade of the screwdriver is held against a live wire the bulb lights up when you touch the handle.

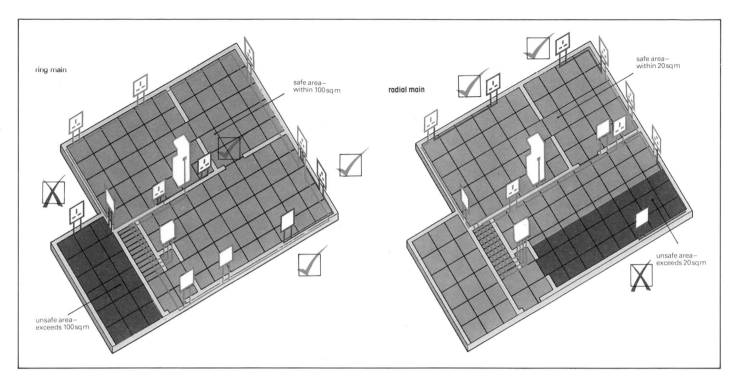

ring main

safe area—
within 100 sq m

radial main

safe area—
within 20 sq m

unsafe area—
exceeds 100 sq m

unsafe area—
exceeds 20 sq m

by the existing circuit must not exceed 20 sq m. Any new socket must be fitted inside this area.

Never draw power from a fused connection unit or from an appliance which has its own individual supply.

Once you have found out whether you have a radial or ring circuit refer to the diagram, then wire up according to the following rules:
• On a radial circuit system draw power only from a socket with one set of wires (that is, the last socket in that circuit).
• On a ring circuit system draw power only from a socket with two sets of wires (that is, a socket not previously added to).

Siting the new socket

The next step is to decide exactly where you want to put your new socket. As a general rule, try to position it at a minimum of 150mm above the level of the floor or worktop and well out of reach of anyone working at a sink.

For flush-mounted sockets and installations where the cable is to be hidden in the wall, you must take into account the type of wall construction. On a solid masonry wall you can fit the socket almost anywhere; but on a timber framed (stud) wall a new crossmember or trimmer needs to be added between two studs to take the backing box. The cable is then fed behind the skirting to the socket.

If you are not certain what type of wall

you are working on, test it by tapping the surface with the handle of a screwdriver a hollow sound will indicate that it is a stud or timber frame construction, a dull thud that it is solid (probably plaster on brick or building block).

If you discover that you are dealing with a frame wall, 'sound out' the whole area you want to work on. By trial and error you should be able to work out roughly where the timber uprights (studs) and crossbearers are sited (bearing in mind that they are probably at rough 400mm or 450mm centres) and mark their positions in chalk across the face of the wall. Once you have a good idea of where you want to install your new outlet, plan the best route to take the cable from there to the socket that is your power source. Run the cable along the top of the skirting board as far as you can. If one of the sockets is higher than the other, avoid the temptation to plan the run so that the cable runs diagonally across the wall—if you do, it is much more likely that someone may accidentally puncture the wires at a later date. Mark out the route, including the new socket position, using a piece of chalk and a wooden straightedge. Measure and note the distance between the outlets.

What you need for the job

As well as the new socket and fixings you will need a length of cable to take power from an existing supply. Ask for 2.5mm² 'twin and earth' and always get a few

metres more than you actually need. You will also need to buy some PVC earth sleeving. This is green/yellow in colour and is used to cover the earth wire and prevent it accidently touching one of the other wires or the backing box. Buy a box of cable clips to hold the cable in place, and a rubber grommet to protect it where it enters the new socket.

Any damaged areas must be made good afterwards with plaster. Use either ready-mixed plaster which you can buy in large tubs from most DIY stores or purchase a small bag of finishing plaster to mix up your own. If you are installing a flush socket in a stud or timber frame wall you will also need a small piece of plasterboard and some clout nails to patch up the damaged wall before you finish it by plastering the cracks.

Starting work

Before you start work, cut the power at the mains consumer unit. Remove the relevant fuse and keep it with you just in case someone switches on the power accidentally while you are working. Just to make sure that you really have cut off the supply, test the existing socket with a mains tester screwdriver or plug in an appliance such as an electric lamp.

Using plastic conduit

Start by fitting the backing box in place using impact adhesive or plugs and screws. Then measure and cut the backing pieces to length—use a junior hacksaw—and fix them in position as you did the box.

Feed the cable into place making sure

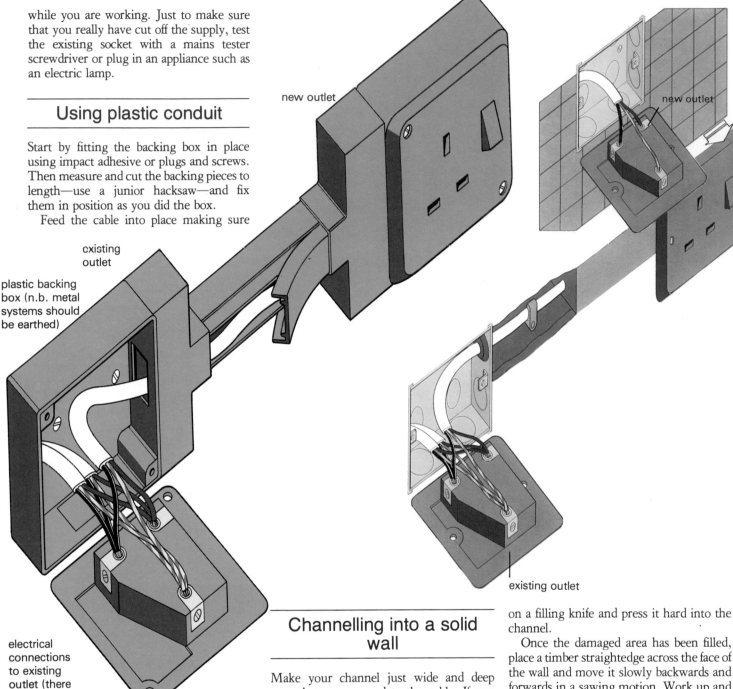

new outlet

existing outlet

plastic backing box (n.b. metal systems should be earthed)

new outlet

electrical connections to existing outlet (there may be either two or three sets of cables)

existing outlet

there are no twists or kinks (some manufacturers supply small clips which are spaced along the top of the conduit to hold the cable tightly). Lead the cable into both backing boxes, strip the ends and make the electrical connections to each socket (see Wiring the sockets).

Trim the conduit covers to length and snap them into place on top of the backing pieces (fit angled adapters as well, if these are supplied). Screw both faceplates into position, then turn the power back on at the mains.

Channelling into a solid wall

Make your channel just wide and deep enough to accommodate the cable. If you are fitting a flush-mounted socket, cut out a recess about 7–8mm deeper than the backing box. Fix the box in place using screws and wallplugs.

Thread a length of cable into the channel and secure it every 300mm with cable clips. Knock out one of the cable entry blanks, add a grommet, and feed the cable into the backing box of each outlet. Strip the cable, bare the wires and attach them to the terminals on both sockets (see Wiring the sockets).

To repair damaged areas, load your plaster onto a small board and stand near the wall. Pick up a small amount of plaster

on a filling knife and press it hard into the channel.

Once the damaged area has been filled, place a timber straightedge across the face of the wall and move it slowly backwards and forwards in a sawing motion. Work up and down the wall so that the plaster is smoothed off neatly. Sand any ridges when it is dry.

Frame wall insulation

On a frame wall, start by cutting away a section of wall boarding around the proposed outlet with a sharp knife and straightedge. The hole should be about 300mm high and just wide enough to half overlap the uprights on either side. Skew nail a trimmer between the uprights to accommodate the backing box then cut a

1 *Cut the chase, angling the chisel in the direction you want to go*

2 *An easy way to cut a recess for the backing box is to loosen the brickwork first by drilling a number of closely spaced holes 7–8mm deeper than the box*

3 *Level the plaster with a straightedge. Draw it back and forth in a sawing motion*

4 *On a frame wall make sure the trimmer is correctly aligned then skew nail it firmly on both sides. Cut a recess for the backing box and screw it to the trimmer. Make sure that the leading edge of the box is level with or just below the original wallcovering*

5 *If you cannot reach the cable when you drop it down the cavity, retrieve it with a piece of coathanger wire*

recess for the box itself with a mallet and wood chisel.

If the existing socket is directly below the new outlet, making the correct electrical connection is relatively easy. Simply drop a length of cable down the cavity. Then remove the existing socket faceplate and backing box and pull the end of the cable through the gap in the wall.

In most cases, however, you will want to lead the cable to an existing socket some distance away. The easiest and quickest way to do this is to drop the cable down the cavity and then lead it behind the skirting board.

Push a bolster or large-bladed

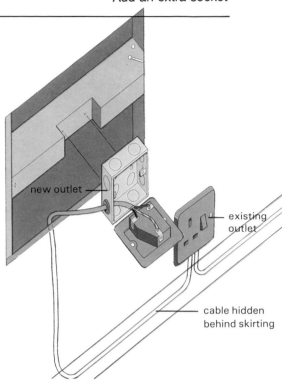

A trimmer is a length of 100mm × 50mm sawn timber nailed between the studs

screwdriver down behind the skirting board and lever it gently away from the wall. Drop the cable down from above and retrieve the end. On most walls there will be a small gap between the wall boarding and the floors—if not, cut away a section with a trimming knife large enough to reach the cable. Then lead the cable along the wall. Secure it with cable clips as close to floor level as possible. This will avoid nailing through the cable when the skirting board is replaced. Make the electrical connections to each outlet (see Wiring the sockets).

Patch up the damaged area around the socket with a small piece of plasterboard. Cut out a small square hole in the middle of the board to accommodate the backing box and nail it to the uprights and to the new trimmer with clout nails. Then make good the area around the socket with filler.

Wiring the sockets

Connect the wires to the back of the faceplate as shown above. Cut off a 55mm length of sleeving and slip it over the end of the bare earth wire. When wiring the new socket (or fused connector) double over the end of each wire so that it is gripped more tightly (and safely) in the terminal.

On the existing socket, twist each pair of wires together with pliers before making the electrical connections to the relevant terminals.

OUTDOOR POWER SUPPLY

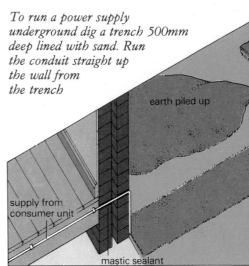

To run a power supply underground dig a trench 500mm deep lined with sand. Run the conduit straight up the wall from the trench

earth piled up

supply from consumer unit

mastic sealant

Taking electricity outside your house opens up a huge number of possibilities. It can be used to run power tools in a garden shed; an electric lawnmower anywhere in the grounds; a battery charger in the garage; fairy lights at the bottom of the garden—or even a stereo system to play sweet nothings to the geraniums in your greenhouse.

But don't underestimate the hazards involved: outside the house, electricity is potentially much more lethal. This is partly because the chances of sockets and other fittings getting wet is much higher—and electricity and water just don't mix. It's also partly because there is more chance of the installation suffering physical damage from wheelbarrows or gardening tools.

For these reasons, the rules governing outdoor electric supplies are usually much more stringent than those for indoor wiring—and you should find out what your local electricity code or regulations prescribe. The details given here are based on IEE Wiring Regulations, used in the UK.

First thoughts

Your first consideration should be what sort of a supply you want, and where. It's a good

idea to be fairly generous in your estimates, and to allow for any expansions and extensions you think you might need. The most time-consuming part of the job is running the cables to where you want them, and installing ones that have enough capacity for any supplies you might want later could save you quite a lot of effort in future years.

There are four main systems you might consider, and they each are wired in a different way.

Sockets outdoors, mounted externally on a house wall: This is the easiest system to install—you can connect it to an existing circuit inside the house—but it is quite restricting.

Lighting and socket outlets in a garage, greenhouse or shed: You must provide a separate circuit for a supply to any detached outhouse. Between the house and the shed (or whatever) the cable can be run either underground, or slung overhead. Though there are special cables for outdoor supplies, it is probably easiest to use ordinary PVC sheathed twin and earth cable, protected if it runs underground in heavy duty plastic conduit.

Armoured PVC cable and Mineral Insulated Copper Core (MICC) cable are

available, but they are expensive and require specialized tools and techniques to connect them to their glands and terminals—definitely a job for a professional electrician. **Other outdoor sockets, mounted throughout the garden:** These are perfectly acceptable providing the sockets are of the waterproof type or in waterproof boxes. Any mounting posts or boxes must be firmly fixed. A separate circuit must be used for these sockets; it must be wired up with PVC cable run through heavy duty plastic conduit and buried in the ground.

Outdoor lighting: It's best if lighting used round the garden, and any pumps used in garden ponds, are run from extra-low voltage supplies: 12V or 24V. These of course need a transformer before they can be connected to the mains supply. Site the transformer in the house or an outhouse, so that all the outdoor cable will be a safe low voltage. Low voltage cables needn't be buried or protected from damage (they aren't lethal) bit it's wise to do so—cutting through a cable is irritating, to say the least.

Types of sockets

• Ordinary plastic sockets, as used in the home, can be used in garages and greenhouses—but they're not the wisest choice as they can be damaged easily. A better choice is an impact resistant, or metal-clad socket—accidental knocks won't damage these robust sockets.

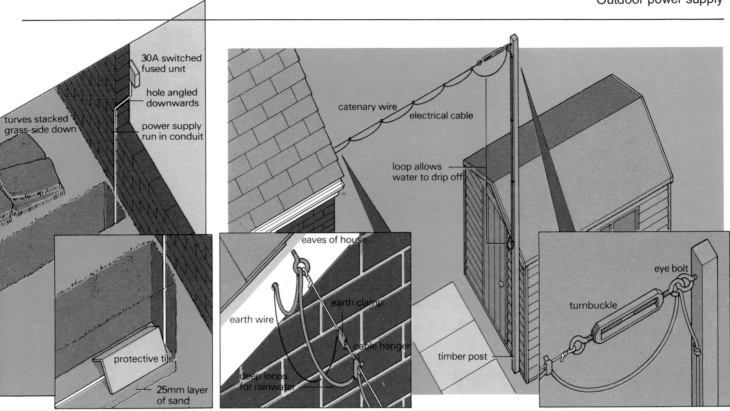

An overhead supply can be erected using easily available materials. Keep it above minimum height and allow loops in the cable for moisture to drip off outside the buildings

• For use externally, but in sheltered conditions, a metal socket with a shower-resistant, splash-proof casing may be enough.

• In more exposed conditions, a metal-clad socket fitted into a totally waterproof housing can be used.

• Special waterproof metal sockets are the alternative. These don't need an extra housing, but they can be used only with special plugs, which you would have to fit to each of the appliances you might want to use in the garden.

• For a socket connected as an extension to an existing internal electrical circuit, you should use a socket fitted with an RCD—see Providing protection—unless the whole circuit is fitted with such an RCD.

Providing protection

For electricity supplies outside, a normal fuse (or even a miniature circuit breaker—MCB) is not enough protection against electric shock—there are many potentially lethal faults that a fuse will not react to, and even for those that it does, it may not blow quickly enough to prevent you from being killed. So all circuits for outside use should be protected with a *residual current device*, or *RCD*. This is frequently known as a current-operated earth-leakage circuit breaker (ELCB).

For a separate outdoor circuit, use a *high-sensitivity* RCD, fitted into just that circuit.

High-sensitivity RCDs will 'trip' with a fault current as low as 30mA—well below the level at which you can get a fatal electric shock. And by confining its action to just the outside circuit, you ensure the whole house isn't cut off whenever it trips—a high-sensitivity device may occasionally trip by accident, or during a lightning storm.

Circuit-protection RCDs are available in a number of current-carrying capacities, from 24 amp to 80 amp. For the usual 30 amp outdoor circuit, use one with a 30 amp rating. For a socket fitted to an indoor circuit but intended for use with outdoor appliances, it may be better to use a socket outlet RCD which protects just that socket: again, you should go for a high-sensitivity (30mA) type.

An RCD is not a substitute for a fuse—note that you will need a fuse or MCB in the circuit as well.

When choosing a site for a RCD or ELCB, consider the rest of the wiring as well: it would repay you to place it between the consumer unit and the company fuse so that all the domestic wiring is protected in the event of an electrical fault developing. Remember, however, that if you intend to place the RCD or ELCB in this position, it's the electricity supply authority's job to make connections to the company fuse—if you are in any doubt, consult them or a professional electrician before commencing work. They may also be able to check your wiring before making final connections to the consumer unit.

Sockets on a house wall

If you have only a small garden, it's worth considering restricting any outdoor electrics to a socket mounted on the house wall—it's much the simplest job to do.

You can connect a socket mounted on the outside of the house wall to an existing ring mainpower circuit, or a radial circuit, if this won't overload it—see Adding to a power circuit.

First (assuming you have a choice) decide whether you are going to connect the extension to a circuit running at ground level, or one running a first floor level. The decision is basically one of convenience. The socket itself should be mounted about 1.2m above ground level, so that it is less likely to be splashed or damaged—in either case, you'll have to run cable up or down the wall.

Choose a position to mount the socket (or sockets, if you're fitting more than one). Then decide on the type of sockets to use—see Types of socket. (When buying, make sure you get any mounting bases, waterproof covers, and so on that you'll need: explain clearly that you intend to mount the socket out of doors.) It's best to have the cable run indoors as much as possible—running it up or down the inside of the wall until it is directly behind the position of the socket outlet. If you can do this, then start by drilling the hole in the wall for the cable. Make it large enough to take a length of plastic conduit (so that the cable won't chafe on the brickwork) and angle it so that the outside is slightly lower than the inside; then no water can drain into the house. Fit the conduit into the hole, then run a length of cable through it. Connect the cable to the socket, and mount the socket on the wall, following manufacturer's instructions. Make sure the socket is fixed firmly: drill into the bricks or stonework rather than the mortar courses, and use proper wallplugs. If your house is clad with weatherboard, still fix the socket to the brickwork beneath. It is wise to seal the joint between the socket and the wall using mastic, to keep out any moisture.

If you want to run the cable outside rather than on the inside, then you should run it through heavy duty plastic conduit. Use proper fittings to joint the conduit to the piece inserted in the house wall. Then fix it securely to the house wall, and carefully feed the cable through. (See Using plastic conduit.)

Run the cable to the point where you intend to connect it to the existing circuit. For wiring under the floorboards, if the cable run is at right angles to the joists, drill the joists at the mid-point of their depth: do not notch the joists. Cable run over walls can be fixed directly to the wall surface, or run in plastic trunking fixed to the wall. Or you can bury it in the wall. To bury cable on a masonry wall, cut a vertical slot (a *chase*) through the plaster to the wall behind. Do this using a sharp, wide chisel—a bolster chisel and club hammer will do, but especially on old, crumbly plaster, an old wood chisel might make a neater job. If you are leaving the cable exposed on the wall surface, clip it neatly into place. If you are burying it in plaster, a few clips will help to keep it flat and clear of the wall surface. You do not need to run it in conduit, but you can do if you prefer.

On a stud wall, you can usually drop the cable down the cavity behind the plasterboard. Finally, make the connections at the joint box or into the back of an existing socket. Switch on again at the mains, and check that everything works properly.

Replace any floorboards, and make good any plaster chases using a proprietary ready-mix plaster or cellulose filler.

Finally, remember that even the most weatherproof of sockets should not be used while it is raining—unless the manufac-

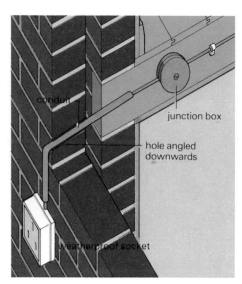

Installing an outside socket can be as simple as one indoors, if you use weatherproof units and prevent water getting into the house

1 *Drill through the outside wall using a masonry bit which matches the conduit—otherwise you'll have to drill from both sides*

5 *Fit the socket face-plate securely and leave the weatherproof cover in place at all times when you're not using the socket*

6 *You can connect to the ELCB yourself, but you must get the electricity supply authority to connect it to the mains supply*

turer's instructions *specifically* say that you can. The most that the majority of weatherproof sockets can offer you is the guarantee that they can be installed safely outside to be used in dry weather.

Adding to a circuit

Ring main power circuit: to install one single or double external socket, the easiest thing to do is to run a branch, or *spur* cable from the ring to the new socket. You can connect the spur cable directly to the back of an existing socket on the circuit, providing this really is on the ring main and not already on a spur (you cannot connect another branch to an existing spur). Or you can connect the spur to a joint box, fitted into a run of cable—again, providing this is actually on the ring, and is not a spur cable. If you want to connect more than one external socket, it is best to break the ring and extend it.

Whatever method you use, wiring is carried out in 2.5mm^2 twin and earth cable. The bare earth wire on each cable must be sheathed with green and yellow plastic.

2 *Run the conduit down to the socket location, fit a conduit adaptor to the socket, and cut the conduit to length*

3 *Feed the electric cable through the conduit from inside the house then fix the socket case in position. Trim and strip the cable cores*

4 *Wire up the socket in the normal way, but make doubly sure the connections are tight and the wires cannot work loose*

7 *An ELCB fitted between the company fuse and the consumer unit will protect the entire house from danger if a fault develops*

A single ring main circuit, and its spurs, should not serve an area greater than 100m², which may restrict the positioning of the external socket; in any case, it is sensible to put the socket as close as possible to the circuit.

Radial circuits: Run a branch cable from the *last* socket on the circuit, to each of the external socket outlets in turn. There is a much greater restriction on the area that radial circuits can serve: a circuit wired in 2.5mm² cable and fused at 20 amps can serve only 20m²; one wired in 4mm² cable and fused at 30 amps can serve only 50m².

Using plastic conduit

Plastic conduit is much like plastic plumbing pipe. It can be bent by hand using bending springs—you may have to *carefully* apply some heat for making tight bends or in cold weather—or you can use elbows. The conduit is joined with push-fit fittings—for use outside and underground, joints should be sealed using a special solvent adhesive.

On long lengths, or at tight bends,

Plastic conduit comes in a range of sizes and diameters with adaptors to suit the majority of fittings such as bends, socket outlets and switches

'inspection' fittings should be used. These have a removable cover so that you can check the cable is being fed through the conduit properly, without strain or twisting. After testing the circuit, covers should also be sealed in position.

Straight lengths of conduit over about 8m long should be joined so that the tube does not buckle or split as the temperature changes. Expansion couplings will need sealing when used out of doors or underground, but use a non-hardening mastic, not the normal solvent.

When buying your conduit, tell the supplier what size of PVC-sheathed cable (and how many, if more than one) you plan to thread through it—conduit comes in a range of diameters.

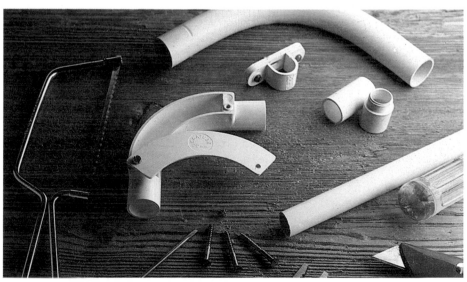

Cables underground

Burying the supply cable gives a neat result, but can be difficult to do under, say, a concrete path. It's also essential to decide at the outset what size of system you want—so you don't need to re-lay the cable later.

Cable run underground should be buried at least 500mm deep—more under flower borders and vegetable plots. It must be protected by running it inside heavy duty plastic conduit. You must cover the conduit with paving slabs or proprietary slabs marked DANGER—ELECTRICITY available from builder's merchants.

Decide where the cable will emerge from the house, and enter the outhouse. Dig a narrow trench between these two points—in as straight a line as possible. The bottom of the trench should be reasonably smooth and soft: if the grounds is full of stones, first lay a 25mm bed of sand.

Assemble your conduit on the surface next to the trench. If the route is long, it may be sensible to thread the cable through each section before you join it to the next. Leave enough cable spare at both ends of the conduit to reach to the first piece of switch-gear—if at all possible, do not have any joints in the cable. For a 30 amp supply, you need 6mm^2 twin and earth cable.

Lower the completed conduit into the trench. The cable must be protected with conduit until it disappears inside the buildings with vertical sections of conduit, properly sealed to the horizontal run in the trench using either elbow fittings or bends. Thread these sections of conduit over the cable, then fix the conduit to the walls.

Pass the cable through the walls, again through properly jointed sections of conduit—see Socket on a house wall.

Don't fill in the trench until you have finished the wiring and tested the supply.

If you are lucky, and your house and outhouse are connected by a brick wall, you can run your cable along this, rather than burying it. It should still be protected inside plastic conduit. You must **not** run cable along a fence—fences can collapse.

Whatever method you use for the cable run, it's best to connect it at the house end to an RCD—which will also act as the isolating switch the circuit needs.

Run the cable from the point at which it enters the house to the consumer unit—see Socket on a house wall. Fix the RCD onto the wall next to the meter or consumer unit following manufacturer's instructions and wire the supply cable to this. Connect the RCD to a new set of metal tails running to the consumer unit. Use a 30 amp fuse (either rewirable, cartridge, or MCB, depending on what your consumer unit is designed to take).

If there's no spare capacity in the consumer unit, connect the RCD to a new switched fuse unit (essentially a single-way consumer unit) and get your electricity board to connect the RCD to the supply.

8 *Decide on the route your trench will follow and mark this out with a string line, avoiding concrete paths and intervening walls*

9 *Dig the trench 500mm deep and fill the base with sand. Assemble and test fit the conduit then run the cable through it*

10 *If you can't get the proper slabs (marked 'DANGER—ELECTRICITY'), use concrete paving slabs to protect the conduit*

11 *Fill in the base of the trench, then fix the conduit to the outhouse wall using saddle clamps before filling and returfing the rest*

Overhead supply

An overhead supply saves you having to dig up gardens and paths, but it can be just as tricky to install as an underground one, and doesn't look so nice.

Overhead cable must be kept at least 3.5m above the ground—5.2m above any driveway. If the house or outhouse isn't high enough, you will have to run the cable between posts either firmly fixed in the ground, or securely bolted to the building.

On short spans of up to 3m, ordinary PVC cable will be able to support itself; on longer spans, you will first have to fix a supporting *catenary* wire, using special eyebolts and straining screws. PVC cable is then slung from this wire.

Start by installing any posts you need to raise the cable. Remember that the cable will sag in the centre of its run—allow an

12 *At the outhouse you can either sink a post in the ground or bolt it to the wall so that the incoming supply cable is at the right height*

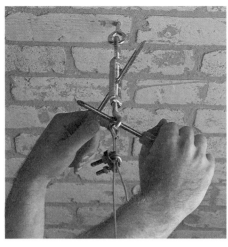

13 *Cut the catenary wire slightly under length, connect it to the turnbuckle, stretch this on the eyebolt and tighten using a screwdriver*

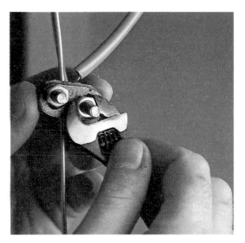

14 *Fix the catenary wire to the turnbuckle using a cable clamp and eye. Use a second cable clamp to secure an earthing wire in to it*

15 *Hang the power cable in loops from the catenary wire using cable ties turned in a figure eight to prevent the cable chafing*

extra 300mm for this.

The catenary itself is a length of galvanized steel wire. At one end, this is firmly bolted to the wall or post. At the other, it is attached to a straining device which allows you to take up any excess slack. The straining device is hooked over an eyebolt fixed to the wall.

To make the loops in the wire requires you to turn the wire round an eye former and secure it with a cleat, both of which are available from hardware stores.

When the catenary is securely fitted, attach the cable to it using cable fasteners at 500mm intervals. At the ends, allow the cable to drop into a loop before passing it through the walls. The loop helps to shake off any rainwater drips that might enter the house or run down the wall. For a 30 amp

supply, use 6mm² twin and earth cable.

The cable can pass into the house or outhouse at this level or you may want to run it down the wall first. As long as it is well above head height, it should not need protection; otherwise, enclose it in plastic conduit to prevent accidental damage.

The catenary itself must be earthed. Connect a separate sheathed earthing wire to the catenary, and run this to the connecting point inside the house.

Connections in the outhouse

It's up to you how you wire up your outhouse. Treat the incoming cable as you

would the 'tails' from the electricity meter inside the house, and follow the normal wiring practice.

In most cases, all you will want in your outhouse is a few socket outlets and a light or two. Providing you have chosen your cable and fuses correctly, then you can connect a radial power circuit direct to an unfused isolating switch rated at 30 amp or more, fitted where the supply cable enters the outhouse. In the radial circuit, put in a fused connection unit (fused at 3 amps) and from this run a normal lighting circuit.

Cable in the outhouse need not be covered but if you think there is any chance of it being knocked or otherwise damaged, then run it in conduit or channelling, or in a trunking system.

If your plans are more ambitous, it would be sensible to connect a small consumer unit to the incoming supply, instead of a simple isolating switch, and run lighting circuits and ring main power circuits off this, following all the usual rules for domestic wiring. If you intend a large-scale installation like this, check how much current it might take—if it's greater than 30 amps, you'll need a larger supply cable, RCDs, and main fuses than those specified in this article.

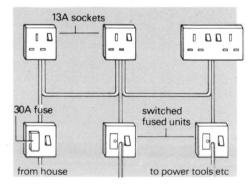

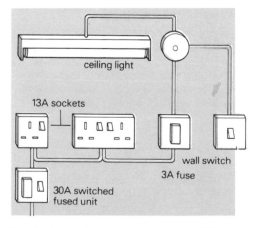

Inside the outhouse protect your radial power and lighting circuit with a 30 amp fuse

FIT A NEW CONSUMER UNIT

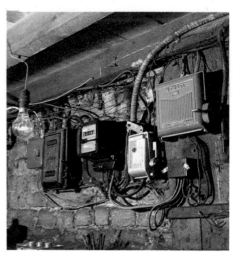

An old electrical installation is typically a jumble of switches and fuse units, with old, decaying cables and inadequate capacity

From cookers to videos, the list of electrical equipment used in the home seems almost endless and it's placing an increasing burden on the domestic electrical system. If the wiring of your house is more than about 25 years old, the chances are that it needs replacing anyway—so you can increase the capacity of the system then. But if your home's wiring is satisfactory, you can increase its capacity simply by installing a new, larger consumer unit.

The job's not especially complicated—more a matter of being careful and methodical about making the connections. And since the final connection to the mains has to be done by the electricity board, you never have to deal with any live parts.

Types of distribution point

In older installations, the house circuits will probably originate from separate switch and fuse units, which allow individual circuits to be isolated from the mains supply. Alternatively, you may have a fuseboard which is controlled by a separate main switch and fuse or individual fuseboards which deal separately with the lighting and power circuits.

But by far the best way of distributing electricity to where it's needed in the house is to use a modern consumer unit containing a number of fuseways and a double pole isolating switch. Both from a safety and practical point of view, modern consumer units have a number of advantages. And if you've got an old distribution system, it's worth bringing it into line with current wiring practice.

On the safety front, old switch and fuse units and fuseboards themselves often have double pole fusing, which means that the live (phase) and neutral of each circuit have separate fuses. It's possible for a situation to arise in which a fault on the circuit causes the neutral fuse to blow but leaves the one on the live side intact: the result is an ineffective safety device, as part of the circuit could still be live. So if you've got double pole fusing it's important for reasons of safety that you replace it.

Consumer units have single pole fusing, which means that the fuse is connected to the live side of the circuit only. When this blows as a result of a fault or an overload all

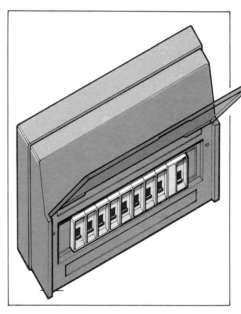

A modern consumer unit consists of a neat plastic or metal box containing all the terminals. All that's visible from the front is a row of MCBs and the main isolating switch; there's a plastic cover over these

power to the circuit is cut off; no part remains live.

But don't imagine that simply fitting a new consumer unit will by itself renew the safety standards of an old wiring system. If the wiring is old, it's potentially lethal. If you intend to upgrade your installation by installing a new consumer unit, then it's **vital** that you inspect the existing wiring very carefully (see Checking the wiring). Unless it's run in PVC sheathed and insulated cable you shouldn't attempt the conversion. Old wiring **must** be replaced in its entirety—for your safety and the fulfilment of legal requirements—and you can then install the consumer unit as part of an overall rewiring job.

Checking the wiring

Before you carry out any electrical work, it's absolutely essential you get to know your wiring system. And top of the list should be a check on the state of the cables themselves. Don't be misled by modern light switches and fittings, square pin sockets and a modern consumer unit. It's not unknown for these parts of a system to be renewed leaving the old cables in place.

If you've got lead or rubber-sheathed cable this will virtually be at the end of its life and will almost certainly need replacing in its entirety. The insulation will have deteriorated almost to dust, which, when disturbed, will leave the cores of the cable exposed and extremely dangerous. A rewire is essential and you can then install a new, larger capacity consumer unit as part of the job.

If you've got grey or white (or possibly the older black) PVC-sheathed-and-insulated two-core and earth cable, then you should be able to upgrade your installation by installing a consumer unit in place of switch fuse units, for example. If you're in any doubt get the wiring checked by the electricity board or a qualified electrician.

Also check for sockets and light fittings with poorly fitting cables and insecure terminal fittings. And make sure that any flexes aren't frayed: if exposed cores should come into contact this could lead to short circuits—and possibly even fires. Attention to detail may prevent accidents later on.

Choosing a consumer unit

It's worth spending a little time and seeking professional advice when deciding what consumer unit is best for your house; individual requirements can vary quite considerably.

From a practical point of view, installing a consumer unit with more fuseways than you require at present will make extending

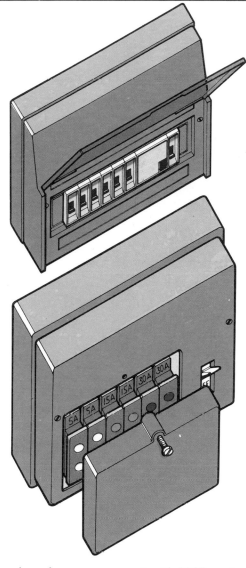

A modern consumer unit with MCBs and ELCBs (above), can detect most faults and shut down the system in milliseconds; a consumer unit with fuses (right) is cheaper but not as efficient

the system in the future that much easier. For example, you may at some time want to run a new circuit to a loft conversion, a back extension or a garage. You could install a modern switch-fuse unit (in effect a mini consumer unit), but the cost, time and extra wiring it entails makes the relatively simple connection to a spare fuseway in a consumer unit a far more attractive proposition. It also contains the connections in one unit— a far more convenient arrangement.

If you've got a fairly new installation, or the house has been rewired recently there'll probably be a consumer unit fitted already. But it's still worth considering whether it's likely to meet your future needs. If not, it'll need to be upgraded.

A standard six-way unit will deal with six circuits. Yet, while it will cope with a basic

installation of two lighting circuits, two power circuits, a cooker and an immersion heater, it's obvious that it's lacking in capacity as far as modern day needs are concerned. However, there are units with far more capacity—some have as many as twelve ways, but eight to ten ways are normally sufficient. If there are fuseways you're not going to use for the time being then fit them with empty fuse carriers, miniature circuit breakers (MCBs)—see Using MCBs and ELCBs—or you can use special blank fuses.

Fuses and circuit breakers

The other important point to consider is whether you want the unit fitted with rewireable fuses, cartridge fuses or with MCBs. The most common types are still the ones fitted with rewireable or cartridge fuses. They give serviceable performance protecting the circuit against faults, overloads and fire risks, as well as giving some protection against electrical shocks.

MCBs are a more expensive alternative but they're a more efficient safety device than fuses, since they respond more quickly to faults.

For example, a fuse rated at 5 amps needs a current of more than 10 amps passing through it (a 100 per cent overload) before it will blow. A cartridge fuse rated at 5 amps will take a current of 7.5 amps (a 50 per cent overload). But best of all is a comparable MCB, which will 'trip' at just over 6 amps (a 25 per cent overload) when there's a fault or an overload on the circuit.

Some consumer units are made specially

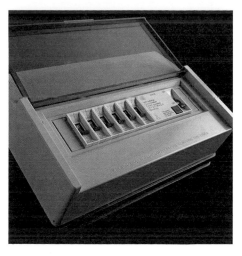

A modern consumer unit containing MCBs with toggle switches and an ELCB for efficient, safe electrification of your home

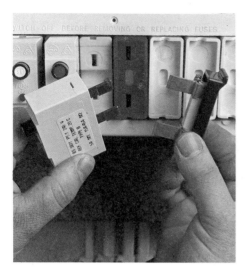

In many consumer units you can replace the rewireable fuses with MCBs, although you'll also have to fit special holders to take the MCBs

to take the traditional type of fuse, and likewise there are units that will take only MCBs. If you already have a consumer unit with fuses you may be able to replace the fuse carriers with MCBs that plug into the fuseways.

The best (but most expensive) consumer units, apart from using MCBs, also incorporate an ELCB (earth leakage circuit breaker—see Using MCBs and ELCBs). This is a sophisticated device, which besides acting as a double pole on/off switch to isolate your supply from the mains, also gives greater protection against the risk of electric shocks and electrical fires than is given by an existing solid earthing system. They're also available as separate units and have to be installed if the electricity board's main earthing arrangements are altered. If you want to fit a consumer unit with an ELCB then it's vital you contact the authorities, who will advise you on the type to use.

Using MCBs and ELCBs

Basically, an MCB is an automatic single pole switch, and the most up-to-date have what's known as a 'high speed current limiting action'.

Inside an MCB there are two mechanisms for cutting off the current. The first is a bimetallic strip. When the circuit is moderately overloaded this heats up, bends and touches a trip bar, which then sets off the trip mechanism, and so renders the circuit dead.

But if there happens to be a short circuit

and a sudden surge of current which exceeds the MCB's rating, then a solenoid activates a plunger, which in turn releases the trip mechanism. Because it operates so quickly (3–5 milliseconds) it shuts down the supply before the fault current has time to damage the installation, hence the description 'current limiting action'.

Once a fuse has been installed in its fuseway, the circuit becomes operational, but this isn't the case with an MCB. This has to be set either by depressing a button or by pushing a toggle switch to the up position. Consequently, you can use an MCB to turn off a circuit without disturbing the other MCBs connected to the consumer unit. You can then work on that circuit safely.

> ### ★ WATCH POINT ★
>
> MCBs and ELCBs incorporate a test button, which you should operate from time to time to make sure they're working. Sometimes the contacts in MCBs and ELCBs can stick if they haven't been 'exercised' regularly.

With MCBs, the circuit that's at fault is instantly recognized because either the toggle switch will have dropped to the off position or the setting button will have been pushed out. And if you try to reset the switch without first correcting the fault the MCB will not function.

Earth leakage circuit breakers (ELCBs) are ingenious devices, which can detect a potentially dangerous earth fault current and turn off the main supply before it has a chance to do any harm. They're used where there's poor mains earthing for an installation. And they also provide greater protection against shocks and fires.

Many electric shocks occur when someone touches a live wire or a faulty appliance resulting in a current passing through the body to earth. But the most sensitive ELCB will trip the shutdown mechanism in less than 30 milliseconds if it detects a current leaking to earth of over 30 milliamps. This is well below the power and duration needed to give you an electric shock.

Similarly, it only takes a small current leaking to earth, even less than 1 amp, to start an electrical fire. But the ELCB will detect this and turn off the supply before the fire can start.

However, ELCBs will not detect live/neutral short circuits or overloads, so they're not a substitute for fuses or MCBs.

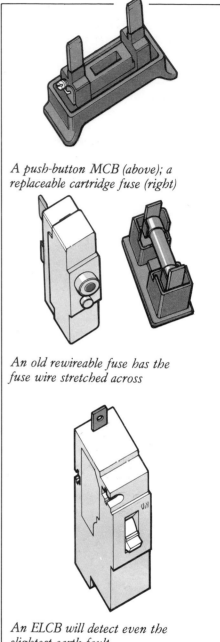

A push-button MCB (above); a replaceable cartridge fuse (right)

An old rewireable fuse has the fuse wire stretched across

An ELCB will detect even the slightest earth fault

ELCBs come as separate units or they can be incorporated in a consumer unit. There are two types: a voltage-operated model and a residual current version, which is also known as a current-operated ELCB. Which type you use depends on local earthing facilities.

The ELCBs incorporated in consumer units are mostly the residual current type. They contain a transformer and a detector winding, which can sense if there's an imbalance in the current between the live (phase) and neutral conductors.

In contrast, the voltage-operated ELCB detects earth fault currents in the earthing circuit itself and will then shut down the installation. But this relies on the earthing system working efficiently, and if the current finds another way to earth, say via metal pipework, then it may go undetected.

Installing a consumer unit

Installing a consumer unit isn't a time-consuming job, nor is it difficult. The only practical skill you need is the ability to strip cable and to anchor the cores properly in their terminals.

What's most important when you're installing a consumer unit is that you work carefully and methodically, running all the cables and their cores to the right place. If you have the slightest doubt about what you're doing, seek professional advice.

For complete safety, get the electricity board to disconnect your supply before you start to carry out any work. You'll need to give them at least two days notice for this, and at that time arrange for the reconnection and a test to be made on the installation. This is a vital check that you've carried out the work properly. Pay particular attention to the earthing of the installation (see diagram opposite). On some units there's still a potential shock risk even with the double pole switch turned off, particularly if the faceplate is removed and you're changing the cable to the new consumer unit. So safety, as always, is the key word.

Replacing fuse boxes: If your circuit wiring is in PVC sheathed and insulated cable and you've got a number of switch-fuse units you want to do away with, then first check what each unit controls and label the cables. Remove the fuses and faceplates from the units in turn to give you access to the terminals securing the live, neutral and earth cores of the cables. On older installations you may find that the lighting circuits don't have an earth core. The wiring regulations now insist that they do, so this is a good opportunity to run single core 1.5mm² green/yellow cable to all the mounting boxes and fittings on the circuit; with all the cables disconnected you can unscrew the units from the back board. Also remove the main switch and fuse unit and any distribution board.

At this stage you'll probably be faced with a confusing array of wires, but if they're all labelled carefully you shouldn't lose track of what you're doing. Because of the positioning of the fuse boxes or fuseboard, some of the cables may not reach to the site of the new consumer unit so you'll have to install junction boxes and

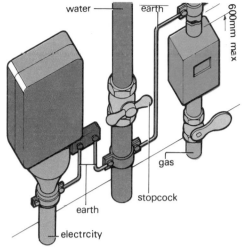

Bond any metal—pipes and radiators, for instance—that could come into contact with electricity to the earth terminal. 'Crossbond' gas and water pipes to earth

extend them. But it's best not to do it yet.

Position the new consumer unit as near to the electricity board's sealed fuse as possible. But if this is in, say, a cellar and you want the unit in a more convenient place you'll have to install a main switch-fuse unit rated at 80 or 100 amps and then run 16mm² two-core and earth cable to the new consumer unit.

When it comes to mounting the unit the best fixing is a fire-proof back board. A piece of 12mm thick fire-resistant chipboard is the best material to use.

Once the unit is firmly in position you can start making the connections. The circuits must be arranged in sequence with the highest circuit ratings nearest the main switch and the lowest furthest away. A common sequence, for example, is to have a 45 amp cooker circuit nearest the switch, followed by 30 amp radial or ring circuits, 20 amp radial circuits (to an immersion heater, for instance) and then the 5 amp lighting circuits.

If you're installing a unit specially designed for MCBs you may have to lift the mounting plate up and out and then take out the busbar so the MCBs can be simply slid along the rail to get the correct order. You don't have to do this with MCBs and fuses that just plug into the unit.

Now you can start to connect up the cables to the terminals in the unit. Work logically beginning with the cooker circuit (if you have one). If the cable won't reach then you'll have to install a junction box and run a cable of the same size to the unit. In this case it could be 4mm², 6mm² or 10mm² two-core and earth cable, depending on your type of cooker.

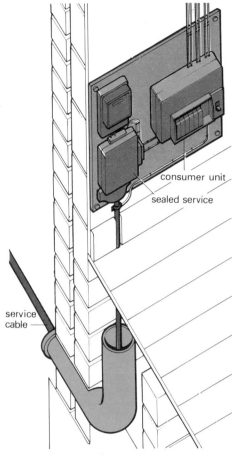

consumer unit
sealed service
service cable

Everything up to and including the meter is the responsibility of the electricity board (top); arrange fuses or MCBs in order with highest loadings next to main switch (above)

At the unit you may have to tap out a knock-out to admit the cable. Modern consumer units are designed with a reasonable amount of space for the wiring up, so don't cut the cores too tightly and avoid making sharp bends in them, which may weaken the insulation and the conductor.

Next strip about 6mm of insulation from the ends of the live and neutral cores and slip a length of green/yellow PVC sleeving over the earth core. Connect this core first to its terminal, then take the black neutral core to the neutral block and the red live core to the top of the fuseway.

When connecting to the terminals, make sure that no bare metal of the conductor is left exposed and it's not good practice to fold over the end of the conductor in a mis-

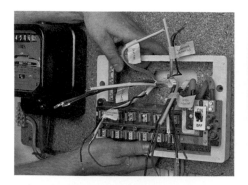

1 *Label and disconnect the circuit cables, remove the old consumer unit and offer up the new consumer unit*

2 *Arrange the cables near their terminals. Try to keep all the wiring as neat as possible*

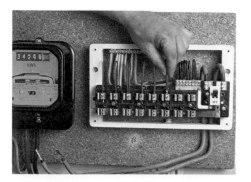

3 *Connect the circuit cores to their terminals in a methodical order working from one side to the other*

4 *Make sure the sleeving is held close to the terminal. Bare wires should not be visible working from one side to the other*

5 *If you're running in a new circuit, feed in the cable and then strip off the insulation*

6 *Arrange the MCB holders in their correct positions and screw the terminals down securely*

7 *Push in the MCBs, replace the unit cover then get the authority to make a test*

guided attempt to get a better fixing.

Repeat this operation for the other circuits, and remember that for ring circuits there'll be two red cores going to the same fuseway terminal.

When all the circuits are in place clip the cables neatly in position and check to see that the sheathing of each cable passes a little way into the consumer unit.

If there isn't going to be an intermediate main switch and fuse, and the consumer unit is right by the meter, then you can connect up the meter tails to the unit and attach the earth core from the electricity board's earthing point. However, if the tails can't be reused because they're not long enough, you'll have to fit red and black 16mm^2 single core insulated cable to the relevant mains terminals in the unit and leave the other ends free for connection to the meter by the electricity board; they can do this when they come to reconnect the supply.

Follow the same procedure if you install a main switch and fuse, but you will be able to link it to the consumer unit using 16mm^2 two-core and earth cable.

If you're just replacing an existing consumer unit with a more modern version, then the wiring is even simpler. Once the electricity board have disconnected the supply, you can disconnect the cables methodically, labelling them as you go. Check that they're in the right order and don't need to be rearranged. Disconnect the power and earth cables from the unit and then fit the new consumer unit in position and replace the wires as before.

There's also another situation where you

may have to install a consumer unit, and that's if you intend to run night storage heaters on an off-peak supply. While you can fit the unit and wire up the radial circuits to the separate heaters, you'll also need a time clock and a special meter, which the electricity board will have to install and connect up.

When the electricity board come to reconnect the supply they may wish to check the earthing of the installation. See page 87 for details of earthing the system.

★ WATCH POINT ★

Allow enough length so that the sheathing can be stripped back about 300mm. Then make a trial run to the relevant terminals and cut the cores to the correct length. You should leave at least 25mm of core on the end of each wire so that it can be gripped tightly and screwed down. Once you have checked the length of the earth cable make sure it is correctly sheathed before fitting.

NEW POWER CIRCUIT

Some people try to get round a shortage of sockets by using multi-way socket adaptors, or worse still by wiring two pieces of equipment to one plug, but these practices are dangerous and can result in electrical fires. If you face this problem, the only safe solution is to extend your existing fixed wiring system.

How you upgrade the circuitry depends on a number of factors. First you must investigate the present wiring. If it's old (run in lead or rubber sheathed cable with sockets that take unfused round pin plugs) don't tamper with it. There's a good chance that the insulation will crumble, leaving exposed live conductors. In this instance a complete rewiring job is necessary, and you will be able to specify as many power points and light fittings as you want. Rewiring a house in full is covered in detail later.

However, homes with wiring less than 30 years old will probably have modern ring circuits, with separate rings for each floor of the house (see All about home electrics, pages 4–6). The usual way of adding extra sockets here is to break into the ring (see Add an extra socket, pages 74–77) but you're restricted with this method as to the number of sockets you can add. If you want to install several sockets, your best option is to supplement the existing circuitry by installing a separate modern *radial* circuit. There's nothing to stop you putting in another *ring* circuit, but this will involve you in extra work and the use of more cable than might be necessary. A 20 amp radial circuit will serve all the socket outlets you need providing they are contained in a floor area of not more than 20 square metres. And using a 30 amp radial circuit can serve a floor area up to 50 square metres. Apart from supplying power to socket outlets, radial circuits can also be used to serve individual high capacity fixed electrical appliances such as cookers and instantaneous showers. Note that the cable size needed depends on the current rating of the circuit and the type of fuse used.

Power for the circuit

Whether you're adding extra sockets or providing power for a fixed appliance via a radial circuit, you must consider how to supply the new circuit with power. If there's a spare fuseway in the consumer unit, you can link the appropriate size cable to this and fit a fuse or MCB of the correct rating.

If your consumer unit has no spare capacity for another circuit, you can always replace it with one that has more fuseways (see: Fit a new consumer unit, pages 84–88). But it may be easier to fit a switch-fuse unit or extra consumer unit alongside the present one. If you intend to add more circuits in the future, a small consumer unit is your best option and you'll have to choose this if you are installing night storage heaters.

Planning the new circuit

If you're installing a radial circuit to provide more socket outlets, you'll be taking a cable from the consumer unit and running it to the first socket, looping from here to the next point and so on until you reach the last one.

First decide where you want the sockets and mark them lightly, in case you have to move them later.

Traditionally, sockets have been set above the skirting about 150mm from the floor, although on very deep skirtings special fittings are sometimes set into them. But there is nothing to stop you siting them higher up the wall.

In kitchens, always keep sockets over 150mm above the work surfaces so they are unlikely to be affected by spills. Never site them over cooker hobs and keep them more than arm's length from sinks.

If you're going to the trouble of installing a new outlet point, it's far more sensible to fit a double socket than a single (unless you're installing a fused connection unit). Switched sockets are useful as you don't have to withdraw the plug to isolate an appliance from the mains.

As with all electrical fittings, buy the best you can. One important point to look for is on the back of the faceplate. Check if there's a metal strap that links the screw holes to the earth point. Its presence means that the screws and the metal mounting box are automatically earthed when the faceplate is fixed on. Cheaper sockets don't incorporate this so you have to earth the mounting boxes separately.

How many sockets you need depends on

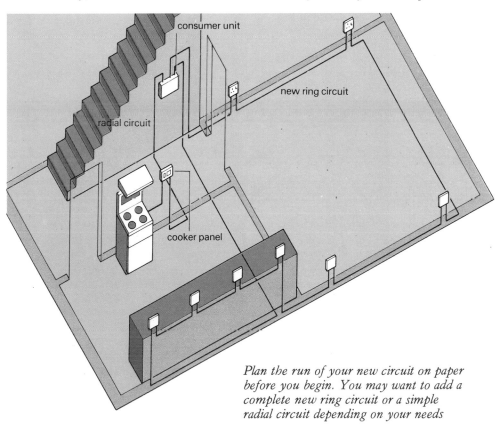

Plan the run of your new circuit on paper before you begin. You may want to add a complete new ring circuit or a simple radial circuit depending on your needs

your existing installation and the electrical equipment you want to use. In kitchens it's often better to install fused connection units to serve some appliances. An *unswitched* fused connection unit is ideal for a freezer as there is no risk of being accidentally turned off except by the freezer's own switch. Fixed appliances like washing machines, dishwashers and waste disposers are best run from their own *switched* fused connection units. The double-pole switch means that they can be isolated from the mains for servicing without having to be disconnected.

Once you've placed the outlet points, work out how to run the cable back from the last point via all the others in turn to the consumer unit or switchfuse unit. It's slightly easier if the circuit serves just one major appliance like a cooker or electric shower. Commonsense, expediency and a willingness to compromise are what's needed. Plan to avoid as many problems as you can foresee, even if it makes the run slightly longer.

The first decision is whether you run the cables on the surface or conceal them wherever possible. Concealing cable runs means cutting some horizontal and vertical chases in the wall—which means a fair amount of making good and redecoration. But you can compromise by surface mounting the run for part of its route before taking it under the floor in some convenient place, inside a cupboard perhaps, and back to the consumer unit.

In a room with a solid floor you may have no choice other than to surface mount most of the run. But in kitchens you should be able to conceal a lot of it behind fitted units and use mini-trunking to disguise the rest.

The alternative with a solid floor is to run the circuit above the ceiling void, then bring the cable down to the socket positions. Again you can use wall cupboards to conceal most of the drops.

Tools and materials

Listing the electrical fittings required is quite straightforward. But make yourself a checklist to ensure you don't forget anything. The biggest problem you're likely to have is in working out how much cable to buy. Measure the proposed run, being generous rather than skimping, and then add a 10 per cent 'detour' allowance. It may also be worth getting a spare junction box just in case you are forced to join two lengths of cable, although you should always try to avoid doing this. Buy plenty of

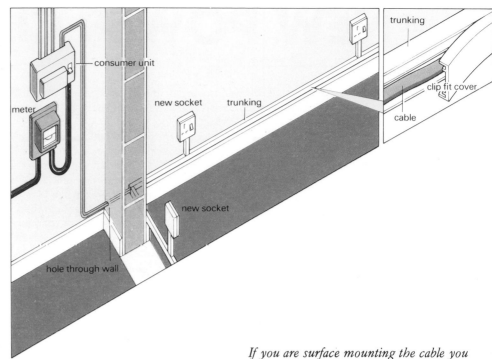

If you are surface mounting the cable you can simplify matters by drilling through a wall to continue the run on the other side. The trunking system consists of a channel and snap-on cover

cable clips for securing the full length of the run.

Simple tools including a screwdriver, wire cutters, a sharp knife, a drill and bits, will see you through most of the work. If you want to cut chases you will also need a cold chisel and club hammer.

Concealing cable runs

Aim for a professional finish when running the cables. It's the only way to blend the additional wiring in with the existing system.

Mark the position of the sockets exactly (use the mounting boxes to draw an outline on the wall), then mark out the proposed route for the cable. Check that horizontal runs don't cross any cables, water or gas pipes already set below the surface. If you can't avoid them you'll have to take extreme care when working near them and you might prefer to consider surface mounting.

Where a cable has to travel some distance up the wall, plumb a line from the socket to the floor. At this point lift back any carpets and raise part of a floorboard to see that there is no obstruction in the subfloor cavity.

Where the cable run has to cross the joists, you'll need to raise a longer length of

floorboard so you can drill a series of holes 50mm below the top of the joists and in the centre of the floorboard run so that the cable is well clear of the fixing nails. A 15mm diameter hole should be sufficient for most cable sizes. However, don't cut the holes at this stage in case you have to change the route later.

With suspended timber ground floors, the gap underneath will enable you to clip the cable to the underside of the joists. There may even be sufficient space for you to crawl underneath which will make the job easier.

Where the cable has runs parallel to the joists, it should be clipped neatly to their sides. Initially, just raise a section of floorboard at each end of this part of the cable run and then check with a mirror and a torch that there is no obstruction to the route from debris left when the house was

★ WATCH POINT ★

For ease of working, and to cause the minimum disruption possible, especially to fitted carpets, plan the run so that it travels round the perimeter of the room even though it may not be the most direct route back to the consumer unit.

★ WATCH POINT ★

★ WATCH POINT ★

Rather than starting to lay the cable at the appliance or socket end, work from where the run goes under the floor. You'll find it easier to push a relatively short length of cable up behind the skirting to the site of the socket instead of having to feed a longer length in the opposite direction.

built or from water or gas pipes.

When you come to laying the cable here you can either pull it under the floorboards using stiff wire, or you can raise some intermediate boards and stretch an arm under the floor to draw the cable along.

Once you've checked the cable run, you can drill the necessary holes through the joists and chop out the chases for the runs down the walls using a bolster chisel and club hammer. Angle the chisel inwards slightly towards the groove you're cutting. By doing this you'll get a much neater edge, particularly if you are working on soft plaster.

If you're flush mounting the fittings, now is the time to chop the recesses and don't forget to channel down behind the skirtings to take the cable below floor level.

After the route has been prepared, you can start to lay the cable. For added protection where the cable is set in the wall, run it in oval PVC conduit, otherwise fix the cable in place with cable clips positioned every 150mm–225mm.

Now work the cable under the floorboards in sections if the run is parallel to the joists and clip it to the sides. You may have to feed it through the predrilled holes or clip it to the underside of the joists.

Surface mounting the cable

Work out and check the route for the cable. It may be possible to drill through the walls to pick up the run in another room, thus keeping the overall route as short and as practical as you possibly can.

Next measure and cut the various sections of trunking you'll need to conceal the wiring. Corners should be mitred, although you can use special internal and external fittings. Drill and plug the fixing holes and then screw the channel section onto the wall, along the top of the skirting and round door and window frames as dictated by the route.

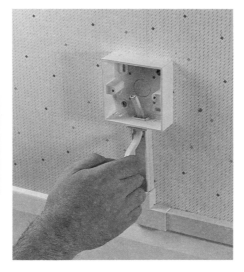

1 *Fix surface mounted boxes carefully, then feed the cable and clip on the trunking cover*

3 *Drill holes along the marks to the depth of the box. Chisel out the rest of the waste*

Now set the cable in the channel and clip on the cover. Remember to leave sufficient cable at the starting point for making the necessary connections.

If you surface mount cable you'll almost certainly be surface mounting the sockets or switch panels, and you can use special adaptors to make a neat join between them.

Fitting the new outlets

How you fit the new outlets depends on the type you are using, but always double check that you are satisfied with their position before starting work.

When you are marking the fixing holes for surface mounted sockets, it's essential

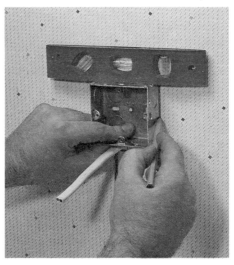

2 *Mark the position of flush mounted boxes using a spirit level to check that they are straight*

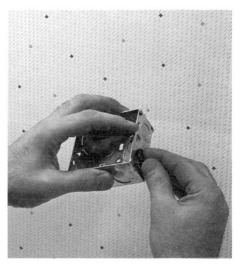

4 *Knock out the cable entry from the box and fit a protective rubber grommet*

that you get the box absolutely level as there is no fine adjustment for getting the faceplate square after the box has been set in place. Next, drill and plug the fixing holes. On a stud wall, if you can't screw into a stud, use cavity wall fixings to hold the box. Before fixing, snap out the cable entry using a small pair of pliers.

Flush mounting sockets

For flush mounted sockets, first check that the wall is suitable. Ideally the wall should be constructed of brick or blocks, though you can recess sockets into a stud frame partition wall. Rest a spirit level on top of the mounting box as you pencil its position on the wall. Next, hold a drill bit against the side of the mounting box and tape the depth of the box on it. Then drill to this depth just inside the four corners of the mounting box's site, and at 2mm intervals along the inside of the guidelines. This will help you chop the recess to the correct depth using a bolster chisel and club hammer. Test with the mounting box at intervals to avoid over-cutting.

★ WATCH POINT ★

If you do over-cut, either pack out the back of the hole with mortar or set the box in place and use extra long screws to reach the fixing holes on the box.

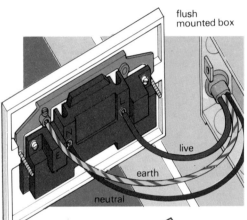

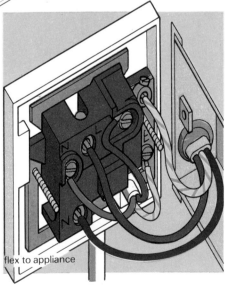

Fix the cores of the cable to the appropriate terminals on the socket faceplate (top). For a fused connection unit (above) or cooker panel (right), connect the cores of the supply cable to the feed side of the box, and connect the appliance flex or cooker cable on to the load side of the box

Mark, drill and plug the fixing holes, tap out the knockout for the cable entry, fit a rubber grommet and then screw the box in place. Don't worry if the box is slightly askew because the adjustable fixing lug allows the faceplate to be straightened.

Feed the 2.5mm² cable (or cables, if the circuit is being continued to another socket) and then strip back about 150mm of sheathing. Sleeve the earth in green/yellow PVC and take off about 6mm of insulation from the ends of the live and neutral cores. Fix these to their respective terminals on the back of the faceplate, and check that you don't have to make a separate earth connection to the metal box. Arrange the cores neatly in the box so they will avoid the fixing screws. Push the faceplate back so that it is flush with the wall and secure.

Fitting a fused connection unit

Fused connection units are fitted in exactly the same way as a socket—they fit onto a single socket mounting box. However, there are special boxes which allow you to fix a fused connection unit directly by the side of a single socket. But you have to run the power supply through one to the other. connections to the appliance go to the 'load'

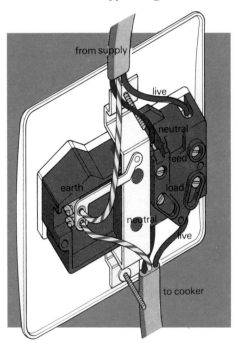

The main thing to remember about wiring any fused connection units is that the circuit cables go to the 'feed' terminals. These are usually the socket type where you just push the exposed cores in and a screw clamps them secure from the side. The flex

terminals. In contrast, these are usually screw down terminals. Wind the flex cores anti-clockwise round the shaft so they are drawn tightly when the screw is tightened.

Mounting a cooker panel

A cooker should be supplied by its own radial circuit run in 6mm² or 10mm² PVC sheathed and insulated two-core and earth cable and protected by a 30 or 45 amp fuse or MCB respectively. Which size of circuit you install depends on the rating of the cooker, anything above 11kW needs the larger circuit.

There are two main types of control panel for a cooker. There is the *cooker panel* which contains a 45 amp double-pole switch for isolating the cooker from the mains and a 13 amp switched three-pin socket. The alternative is the *cooker switch* which just contains a 45 amp double-pole switch. Both are connected in exactly the same way and can either be flush or surface mounted. But for flush mounting remember that the control needs a deeper recess than the ordinary 13 amp socket.

Installation is very similar to fitting a fused connection unit, except that this time you use the same size cable to feed the cooker as you do to supply the control. The supply to the cooker can either be chased into the wall and then fed through an outlet plate below worktop height and connected to the cooker, or it can be run via a connection block if you find it easier to run the cable in two sections. In any event, the cooker panel or switch shouldn't be more than 2 metres away from the cooker.

Set the mounting box in the wall, with grommets protecting the cable entry points. Make sure the box is set square as there are no adjusting lugs. Feed the circuit cable and cable to the cooker into the mounting box and prepare their ends. Remove the faceplate from the panel and then connect the circuit cable to the mains side of the unit. Next connect the cooker cable to its terminals and then run an earth core from the terminals on the mounting box to the earth terminal on the switch. Finally fit the mounting box and faceplate.

The connections at the cooker end are equally straightforward. If you run one length of cable to the cooker, all you have to do is remove the back panel from the cooker to give access to the terminals, then prepare the cable ends and connect them to those terminals. If you install an intermediate connection unit all you have to do is link the cores to the appropriate terminals.

Powering the circuit

Power for the new circuit can be taken from the existing consumer unit or a new unit. Which you use depends on your circumstances, but in all cases turn the power off before connecting into the existing system.

The rating of the fuse or MCB that you have to fit to protect the new circuit will govern where the fuseway should be positioned in relation to other fuseways. The larger the rating, the nearer to the double pole main switch it should go. A common arrangement is a 45 amp cooker circuit, two 30 amp ring circuits, a 30 amp circuit for an instantaneous water heater, a 15 amp circuit for an immersion heater (when the heater is rated at 3kW or higher) and two 5 amp lighting circuits.

In order to make space for the new fuseways, you may have to rearrange the existing MCBs or fuseways. Depending on the type of consumer unit you've got, you may either have to remove the busbar and slide the fuseways along the mounting bar to provide a slot, or, if the fuseways aren't manoeuvrable, you'll have to reorder the live cores going into them and then change the position of the fuse-carriers accordingly.

Feed the cable into the unit and cut it back until you have 200mm spare to work with. Strip the sheathing right back to free the cores and then sleeve the earth core in green/yellow PVC. Then connect the earth to the earth block. Strip off 6mm of insulation from the ends of the other cores and take the black core to the neutral block and the red to the live terminal at the top of the spare fuseway or fitted MCB. Make sure no bare metal of the core is left exposed. Next fit the cover back onto the consumer unit and press in the fuse-carrier or MCBs.

Fitting a switchfuse unit

A switchfuse unit is just a very small consumer unit containing one, or perhaps two, fuseways. Fitting one is a two stage operation—first you have to wire in the new circuit and then the unit has to be connected to the mains supply.

Remove the faceplate from the unit to reveal the fixing holes and screw the unit to a fire-resistant backboard.

The new circuit connections are identical to those for a consumer unit with the cable being fed through a knockout in the top of the unit protected by a rubber grommet. The red core goes to the live, the black to the neutral block and the earth core goes

5 *You may have to rearrange your consumer unit to accommodate the new circuit*

7 *Position the distribution board between the consumer unit and the new switchfuse unit*

★ WATCH POINT ★

Ideally, mount the board on blocks. This will keep it away from the wall and reduce the dangers of damp.

to the earth terminal.

The second operation is to get power to the switchfuse unit. Because this entails working on the supply side of the installation it means that you can only do part of the work yourself. The electricity authority **must** make the final connections.

Essentially, what happens is that the power supply is divided into two after it leaves the meter with a feed going to the consumer unit and another to the switch-fuse unit.

What you can do is fix the distribution board next to the switchfuse and then link this to the terminals of the unit using red, black and green/yellow 6mm² single core cable. The authority must make the final

6 *Fix the new switch fuse unit to a fire resistant board and wire the circuit into it*

8 *Wire the unit to the distribution board and have the authority make the final connection*

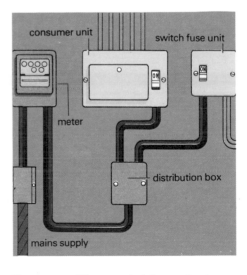

If you are adding a switchfuse unit, the supply will be split at a distribution board

connections to the mains. With the power off they disconnect the meter tails and run them to the distribution board, before connecting the distribution board to the consumer unit.

REWIRE YOUR HOUSE

electricity authority may provide a minimal supply to give you some light and power while you do this. If you are already living in the house, the work will have to be planned carefully so that you can cook, eat, wash and see while you're doing it.

At this stage you must decide how many circuits you are going to have. Since 1947, houses in the UK have been wired with ring mains for sockets and radial circuits for the lights (see pages 4–6). Each floor of the house usually has one power circuit supplying the sockets and one lighting circuit. It may, however, be better to have a separate power circuit for the kitchen since this is an area which uses a lot of electricity.

Planning a lighting circuit

The maximum number of lighting points allowed on a lighting circuit is 12, assuming that each has at least a 100 watt bulb. Where there are more lights than this on your plan or where the total load exceeds 1,200 watts, you will have to have more circuits to cope with the extra load.

Much of the work involved in re-wiring is well within the competence of the average handyman: it involves jobs like lifting floorboards, making holes in joists and walls and screwing things together. But you need to know what you are doing to avoid the two main risks of electricity: electric shock and fire. The first is avoided by *never* working on live circuits or equipment and by having proper insulation and earthing; the second by understanding how to choose the correct cable sizes and components and how to design the system to minimize fire risks, which includes choosing the correct fusing. However, if you're in any doubt about your electrical competence, don't attempt the work: employ a professional. It's not an area where any risks should be taken.

First considerations

The decision to rewire your house is not one to be taken lightly. If the electrical system is faulty it should be replaced as a matter of urgency, but the job involves a considerable amount of upheaval and will take some time to complete satisfactorily. First of all assess the state of your wiring.

There are several ways of recognising old wiring. The first is a number of separate fuse boxes near the meter, some of which may serve only a single socket. Most modern wiring systems have a single fuse box—called a consumer unit (see pages 4–6)—but even if you have one of these, it doesn't mean that the wiring has been replaced. The same applies to sockets and switches—new ones don't guarantee that you have new wiring.

So the next thing is to turn off the electricity at the mains switch or switches and have a look at the wiring itself. The easiest places to look are behind switches and sockets and in the loft space where the upstairs lighting circuit will be. It's easy to tell the difference between cable with shiny sheathing and PVC insulation and that with old, dull rubber—apart from the appearance, the latter will probably be crumbling and cracking and should be replaced.

The first decision is *when* you should rewire. If you're buying a house (and it's essential to look at the electrical system before buying a house), the best time to rewire is before you get all the carpets down and the furniture in place. It's even better if you can do it with the house empty—the

1 *Old rubber-sheathed single core cables must be replaced with new PVC-sheathed and insulated cable. Do this as soon as possible*

2 *Old-fashioned fuse boxes with double-pole fuses can be dangerous; replace them with a consumer unit when you rewire the house*

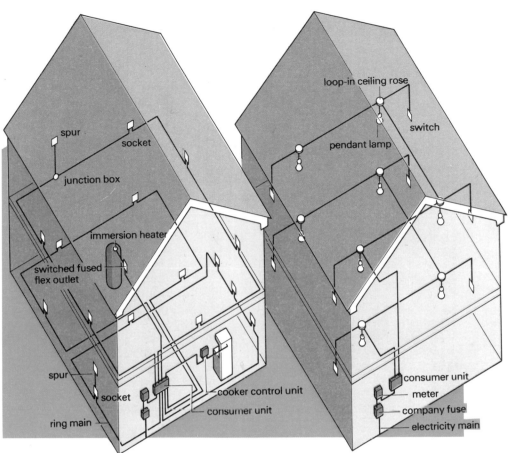

Ring main power circuits (left) and loop-in lighting circuits (right) are the ideal you should aim for when you plan to rewire your house or flat

3 *If you have to do this to your sockets, you don't have enough of them; you may be dangerously overloading an old radial circuit*

There are two methods of wiring lighting circuits: junction box and loop-in. Both use 1.0mm² or 1.5mm² cable protected by a 5 amp fuse and are wired as a radial circuit—the power is supplied from the consumer unit via a cable that runs from one light to the next. The difference between the two types is that with junction box wiring, the cable connects a series of junction boxes with separate cables running from each junction box to its respective light switch and ceiling rose, while with loop-in wiring the supply cable connects the ceiling roses with just one cable going from each ceiling rose to its own light switch (in other words, the roses themselves act as junction boxes).

Junction box wiring requires ceiling roses with two terminals and an earth terminal; loop-in wiring needs ceiling roses with three terminals and an earth terminal. Usually the roses you buy can be used for both—you just use the appropriate terminals in each case.

Each method has its advantages and disadvantages: loop-in wiring uses more cable but you save on junction boxes; junction boxes are easier to wire (working on your knees in the loft) than loop-in ceiling roses (above your head in the room) but are more difficult to get at later. For most installations, you will probably use cable most economically if you mix junction box and loop-in wiring methods on the same circuit.

As well as deciding which wiring system to use, you will also have to decide which method or methods you are going to use to run the cable along the ceiling and down the walls. For ceilings, the best thing to do is run the cable between and through the joists in the ceiling space. For walls, you can run cables directly on the surface with mini-trunking, bury it in the plaster or, with hollow stud partition walls, run it behind the plasterboard.

The third decision concerns the number and types of light fittings you have. You shouldn't forget that table, bedside and standard lamps run off the *power* circuit when planning your overall lighting so that you can decide how many fixed lights you want and where you want them. There is a wide choice of lighting fittings, including plain and decorative pendant lights, track lighting, spot lights, wall lights, downlighters, fluorescent lights and so on. Some of these will need special fittings—some decorative pendants, for example, need something more substantial than a ceiling rose to hang from (see pages 19–22).

Replacing the lighting circuit is an ideal time to think about changing the switching arrangements. Apart from altering the position of individual light switches, you might also want to introduce dimmer switches (remember that fluorescent lights need special dimmer switches) or to have two-way switching of, say, hall and landing or bedside lights. Intermediate switching (operating lights from more than two positions) is also possible and there may be opportunities for operating two or more lights from the same switch position.

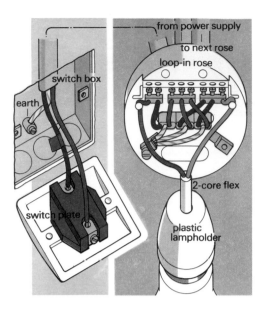

Loop-in connections at a ceiling rose: if the lampholder has metal parts, its flex should have an earth core which is connected to the rose

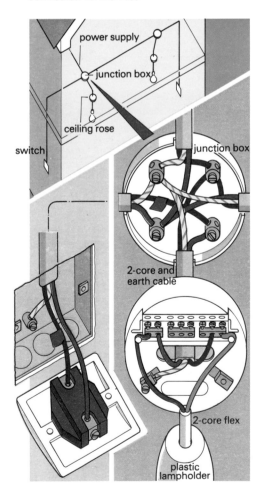

In certain circumstances junction box lighting circuits may be the only answer; you can wire these up by using loop-in ceiling roses

Details of the wiring for all these will be given later.

Finally you should consider what, if any, extras you want to run from your lighting circuit. Typically these might include outside lights, porch lights, electric clocks, extractor fans for the bathroom or kitchen and, possibly, shaver sockets for the bathroom or elsewhere. Check that these won't overload the circuit.

Planning the power circuits

There are two types of power circuit, too: the radial circuit and the ring circuit. Your choice will be dictated by your needs.

With a radial circuit, just one cable goes from the consumer unit to feed the sockets or other appliances on the circuit; with a ring circuit, two cables go from the consumer unit (from the same live terminals)—one to the first socket or fused connection unit in the circuit, the other to the last one. All the intervening socket outlets are connected together in turn in a complete ring. This means that the current is shared by the two cables and a greater load can be carried.

The UK wiring regulations specify one type of ring circuit and two types of radial circuit. Ring circuits must be wired with cable of at least 2.5mm² and can serve an area of up to 100 square metres when protected by a 30 amp fuse or miniature circuit breaker (MCB). One radial circuit, protected by a 20 amp fuse or MCB and wired in 2.5mm² cable, can serve an area of up to 20 square metres; the other, wired in 4.0mm² can serve an area of up to 50 square metres when protected by a 30 amp cartridge fuse or MCB (but *not* a 30 amp rewireable fuse).

The restriction by area rather than by the number of sockets is based on the assumption that you will only use so much power within a given living area at any one time.

As mentioned above, it may be sensible to give the kitchen its own circuit. Not only does this allow for the growing number of kitchen appliances available (many of which, like washing machines, chip friers, kettles and tumble driers have built-in heaters) but also allows you to protect this circuit with an earth leakage circuit breaker (ELCB) which considerably reduces the risk of receiving an electric shock.

For each room in the house, work out the number of socket outlets you think you might want (none are allowed, of course, in bathrooms) and the number of fixed appliances (heated towel rails, extractor fans, washing machines and so on) that you

might want to run off the ring circuits.

Don't skimp on the number of socket outlets: it costs little to have a few extra and it's much better to have too many than not enough. Remember that you're designing for the life of the system and that the number of electrical appliances in use is likely to go on increasing.

As a guide, the following number of outlets (a double socket counts as two outlets) should be adequate to avoid using adaptors and having trailing flexes:
• Living rooms—8 or 10.
• Bedrooms—6 or 8.
• Halls/landings—2 or 4.
• Kitchens—10 or 12.

On the point of boxes, you will need to decide whether to have your sockets (and, for that matter, light switches) surface-mounted or flush-mounted. Flush-mounted

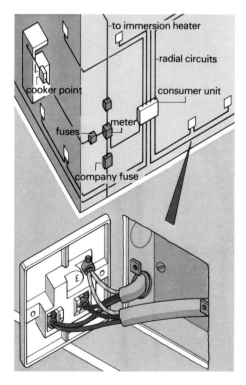

Sockets on a ring main have one cable going in and one coming out; sockets at the end of a spur have only one cable going in

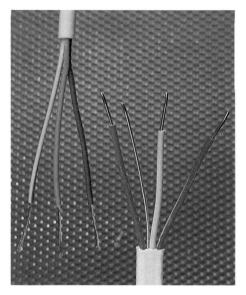

4 *Two types of wire: 0.5mm² two-core and earth flex for pendant lights, and three-core-and-earth cable for two way light switching*

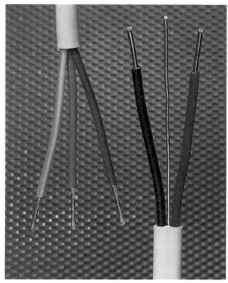

5 *Power circuit wiring: 2.5mm² two-core-and-earth cable for ring mains, and three-core heat-resistant flex for immersion heaters*

Other circuits

The other circuits you're most likely to want are a cooker circuit, an outside circuit and a circuit to supply an immersion heater or an instantaneous electric shower.

A *cooker* has its own supply from the consumer unit which goes to a cooker control unit positioned within reach of the person using the cooker. This has a switch to turn the supply to the cooker off and, sometimes, a 13 amp socket as well though this is not generally a good idea because it invites flexes trailing across the hob. From the cooker control unit, cable is taken to a cable outlet box positioned on the wall behind the cooker where a further piece of cable connects to the cooker itself (the only instance where cable, not flex, can connect an appliance to the mains). The fuse rating at the consumer unit will depend on the maximum capacity of the cooker: for cookers up to 12kW a 30 amp fuse and

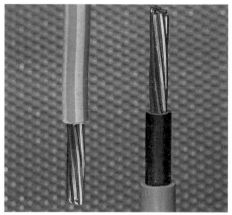

6 *Single core earth cable, and double-insulated cable for meter tails: this has a colour-coded inner sheath in red or black*

7 *Fit an earth-leakage circuit breaker (ELCB) between the electricity meter and the consumer unit for added protection*

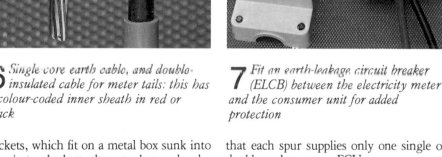

8 *Power circuit hardware: cooker point; one- and two-gang sockets; flex outlets, junction boxes, and socket boxes of varying depths*

sockets, which fit on a metal box sunk into the plaster, look much neater but are harder work as they involve making quite a big hole in the wall and chasing the circuit cable into the plaster. Surface-mounted sockets, which fit on to a plastic box secured to the wall surface, are more obtrusive but you can use cable run on the surface in plastic mini-trunking.

Fixed appliances can be run from fused connection units (FCUs) on the power circuit, either via a flex connected into the FCU or via a flex outlet box. Fused connection units and sockets can also be run as 'spurs' from a ring circuit provided the number of spurs does not exceed the number of sockets or FCUs on the ring and

that each spur supplies only one single or double socket or one FCU.

Bathroom circuits: There are quite specific regulations in the UK covering the use of electricity in any room containing a bath or a shower. The main rules are:
• No socket outlets are allowed.
• No portable appliances are allowed.
• No switches (except cord-operated type) may be within reach of bath or shower.
• Lampholders must be the all-insulated type with a protective skirt, or else fully enclosed fittings must be used.
• Shaver sockets can be fitted, but only the type with an isolating transformer.
• All exposed metalwork must be cross-bonded to earth.

6mm² cable is used; for cookers more powerful than this a 45 amp fuse and 10mm² cable is used. Even if you have a low-powered cooker, it might be sensible to put the higher rated circuit in to cope with any future changes. A split-level cooker can be wired from one control unit provided both parts are within two metres of it.

The UK wiring regulations require that all new sockets installed to supply power *outside* are protected by an earth leakage circuit breaker and are marked 'FOR EQUIPMENT OUTDOORS'. If the socket is inside the house on a ring circuit, it can have an ELCB incorporated in the socket itself; if you're putting in a circuit for an attached workshop or garage, an ELCB

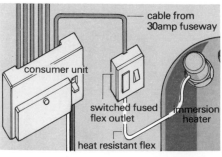

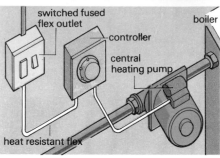

Two common circuits to fixed appliances: in each case use a switched fused connection unit to terminate the fixed wiring and heat-resistant flex running to the appliance

should be fitted to protect the whole circuit. This can be mounted in its own enclosure separate from the consumer unit or can be part of the consumer unit—make sure you choose a unit with enough room for the ELCB to be included and mounted neatly to one side.

Circuits for sheds and workshops not connected to the house or circuits for the garden itself need special precautions to protect them from damage—see pages 78–83.

A circuit for an electric *shower* unit needs to be able to cope with the full rating of the shower. Provided this is 7kW or less a 30 amp fuse can be used, with cable of 6mm^2 if a rewireable fuse is used, or 4mm^2 if a cartridge fuse or MCB is used. The cable is run from the consumer unit to a ceiling-mounted pull-cord double-pole switch and then to the shower.

In many electrical installations an *immersion heater* is supplied off one of the ring circuits, but it should have its own circuit wired in 2.5mm^2 cable and protected by a 15 amp or 20 amp fuse. The cable is taken from the consumer unit to a 20 amp double pole switch (ou can get special ones marked 'water heater'). A timeswitch can usefully be wired into the circuit between the double pole switch and the immersion heater. The flex to the heater should have heat-resistant sheathing and should be open to the air.

Earthing

Traditionally, domestic earthing was supplied via the mains water pipe. But with the increasing use of plastic for water pipes, this can no longer be relied on and most electricity authorities supply a terminal connected to the sheathing of their supply cable from which a 6.0mm^2 single-core cable is run to the consumer unit to provide earthing. In some rural areas and old installations, however, it is necessary to supply a separate earth via an earthing rod and a voltage operated ELCB.

Your electricity board will tell you if they operate *protective multiple earthing*. This means that they may have special requirements for the connections to the mains and for the size of conductors used in *cross-bonding*, where all metal supply pipes and all exposed metal in the house should be connected to the earthing point for safety.

Wiring

There are, in the UK, complicated rules for working out the sizes of cables you should use in different circuits.

This is because the temperature a cable can reach will depend not only on how much current is flowing through it, but also on how well the heat can escape. The things that affect this are the way the cable is run, the presence of thermal insulation, and the temperature of the air surrounding the cable.

Cable run in conduit or in trunking can carry less current than cable run on the surface or buried directly in the plaster. If the cable is in contact with thermal insulation, a larger size should be used (1.5mm^2 rather than 1.0mm^2 for lighting cable in the loft, for example). You should avoid running cable in direct contact with polystyrene insulation and within the airing cupboard and also avoid running it in bunches through holes in the ceiling or wall—keep each cable at least one cable's width from its neighbours.

All connections must be in non-combustible enclosures—mounting boxes and pattresses, for example.

In the UK the electricity authority owns the equipment up to and including the meter. The rest of the installation is your responsibility—and you do not need their permission to alter or extend it. However, they will want to test and inspect it before they connect electricity to a new installation.

You will need to tell them what the likely maximum load of your installation will be.

Fusing

In any circuit there will normally be three fuses. The first line of defence is the fuse in the plug (or fused connection unit) which is rated usually at 3 amps or 13 amps. The second line of defence is the circuit fuse—5, 15, 20, 30 or 45 amps depending on the circuit—and, finally, there is the electricity authority fuse. This is rated at 100 amps and should *never* be tampered with. The fuses are there to prevent excess currents flowing in the wires and thus causing them to overheat. The fuses in the consumer unit are colour coded for the different ratings. Rewireable fuses are the most common and are the cheapest, but they have the disadvantage that they require a current somewhat higher than their actual rating to make them blow. This can sometimes mean that you have to use larger cable in the circuits they are protecting, which isn't a good thing. Cartridge fuses (similar to the fuses used in plugs) blow nearer to their rated current, but the most convenient of all is the miniature circuit breaker (MCB)—a small switch which trips off at a current only slightly greater than its rating and is easy to reset.

Tools and materials

Before starting work, you will need to make sure that you have all the proper tools, equipment and electrical fittings.

You will need two tool kits—an electrical one and a builder's one. The electrical kit should contain:
- Wirestrippers (adjustable ones).
- Wire cutters (diagonal cutters).
- Pliers (two pairs—long-nose and general-purpose).
- Screwdrivers (100mm and electrical).
- Handyman's knife for stripping cable sheathing.
- Red PVC insulation tape.

The building kit should include:
- Electric drill and masonry bit.
- Wood-boring bits (for making holes in joists).
- Bolster and 6mm cold chisel.
- Hammers (club and claw).
- Screwdriver (150mm).
- Floorboard saw.
- Filling knife and wall filler.
- Small spirit level.

In addition, you need protective clothing,

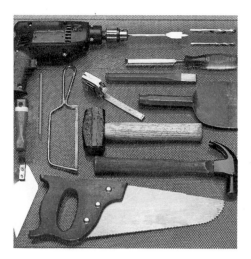

9 *You will need several everyday tools to carry out a rewire — a drill, hammers, saws, chisels, bolsters and measuring tape*

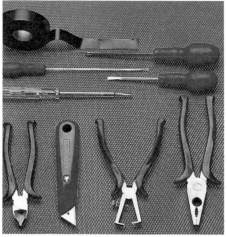

10 *Make a detailed shopping list — cable, wiring accessories and consumer unit — and get several quotes before buying*

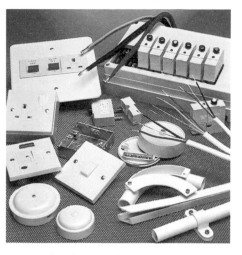

11 *For the actual connection work, you need screwdrivers, wire strippers, side cutters, a sharp knife and some PVC tape*

particular knee pads for working in the loft (and a face mask if it is dirty).

You will also need to find a good source for buying electrical accessories. Compare prices in your local DIY superstores and electrical wholesalers. Use the following as a checklist—you will need to work out the precise quantities yourself:

- **Consumer unit**—at least 8-way, preferably with cartridge fuses or MCBs and perhaps an ELCB as well.
- **Cable**—cheaper in reels for lighting (1.0mm² or 1.5mm²) and ring circuits (2.5mm²); buy only as much as you need by the metre for other circuits.
- **Sockets**—buy double sockets with switches (sometimes cheaper in packs of 5 or 10).
- **Light switches**—one or two gang.
- **Boxes** for light switches—plaster-depth (16mm) boxes should be adequate for most flush light switches.
- **Lamp-holders**—choose heat-resisting kind, and enclosed type for bathrooms.
- **Ceiling roses.**
- **Junction boxes**—5 amp four-terminal for lighting: 30 amp three-terminal for ring circuits.
- **Fused connection units** for fixed appliances.
- **Cooker control unit and cable outlet box.**
- **Immersion heater switch.**
- **Flex** for pendant lights (0.5mm² round two- or three-core, depending on fitting).
- **Cable clips** (different sizes for each cable size being used).
- **Grommets** for metal boxes.
- **Green/yellow PVC sleeving** for covering bare earth wires inside boxes.

- **Special single-core cable** for earth connection (6.0mm²) and for meter tails (16.0mm²).
- **Three-core and earth cable** for two-way lighting and running two lights from one (2-gang) switch.
- **Conduit or mini-trunking.**
- **Clock connectors** for clocks/extractor fans.
- **Special boxes** (architrave boxes or BESA boxes for mounting wall lights).

The final thing you will need is some kind of continuity tester for making sure that connections are intact. You could use a multimeter or make up your own tester with a battery and a light or buzzer.

Starting work

Assuming that the whole house needs rewiring, the work should be divided into four stages: the upstairs lighting (working from the loft), the downstairs lighting and upstairs ring circuit (first floor floorboards up), the downstairs ring circuit (downstairs floorboards up) and finally any special circuits such as cookers, immersion heaters, etc.

You will have to decide at what stage to fit the new consumer unit (if you need one): with whole house rewiring, it's probably best to fit it immediately after the upstairs ring main, connecting the two lighting circuits to the existing fuse boxes as you go.

Depending on the present wiring arrangements, you might also want to fit the cooker and immersion heater circuits just before (or at the same time as) fitting the new consumer unit so that you have hot water and cooking facilities.

Rewiring lighting circuits

Whether you're fitting loop-in or junction box wiring, the procedure is much the same—you simply work from one room to another.

In the planning stages you should have decided where in each room you want the lights and where you want to position the switches, as well as choosing the type of light fitting and switch.

Removing old wiring

After isolating the circuit from the supply (*remove* the fuses—don't just switch off at the fuse boxes) and checking that all the lights are dead, the first thing to do is to disconnect all the light switches and light fittings. Be careful when unscrewing old ceiling roses—you could bring down some of the plaster as well. Remove any wooden mounting boxes that you come across.

Next go up into the loft and unclip the cables from the rafters or disconnect the lengths of metal conduit—you'll have to cut through the cable inside to do this. If there is metal conduit chased into the walls of the room below, it may be much easier to use this for running new cables to light switches: before pulling the old cable out of these, tie a piece of wire or thin cord to the cables at the top of each conduit run.

The cord is attached to a new length of cable which will be drawn down from the loft later on. Make sure that the top and bottom of the conduit are protected by a bush to prevent the cable from chafing.

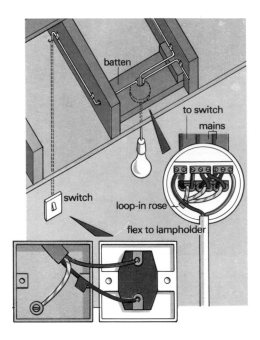

With loop-in wiring, the circuit cable runs from rose to rose. Each rose is linked directly to the switch controlling it

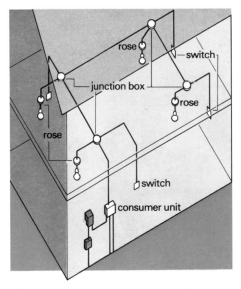

With junction box wiring, the cable runs from box to box. From each junction box separate cables then run to the ceiling rose and switch

There should be a length of conduit to each switch, and one more from the fuse box to the loft. Otherwise, you'll have to chase holes in the plaster for flush-mounted switches or run trunking for surface-mounted ones.

The next thing to do is to mark the position of all the light fittings and switches on the ceilings and walls. For ceiling-mounted lights, drill a small hole from the room below so that you can locate their position in the loft.

You may find that the old ceiling lights were simply screwed to the laths of a lath-and-plaster ceiling—don't copy this, but rather secure the new rose either to a joist or to a piece of wood fixed between the joists. A firm fixing is essential.

Wiring up

With loop-in wiring, the supply cable goes straight to the position of the first ceiling rose or enclosed light fitting; with junction box wiring, it goes to the first junction box—these form an inner 'circle' inside the circle formed by the ceiling roses.

There will be three cables into each loop-in ceiling rose, four into each junction box: supply IN, supply OUT and the cable to the SWITCH, plus supply to the LIGHT with junction boxes. The four terminals are connected as follows:
• **live** wires (red) of IN, OUT and SWITCH
• **neutral** (black) of IN and OUT (+ neutral supply to light)
• **live return** (black) from the SWITCH (+ live supply to the light)
• **earth** wires for all three cables (+ earth to light).

With loop-in wiring, the terminals may be in blocks with the correct number of holes for the number of wires—the light is connected via its flex to the two outer terminal holes. With junction box wiring, a fourth cable is run from the junction box to the ceiling rose where the flex is connected to the cable in the terminals: brown to *live*, blue to *neutral* and yellow/green (where appropriate for metal fittings) to *earth*.

All bare earth wires in junction boxes, ceiling roses and switches should be covered with yellow/green sleeving. The black *live return* from the switch should be marked at both ends by wrapping a small piece of red insulating tape around it to show that it is in fact a live wire.

The switch connections for one-way single-gang switches are the same with either method: the switch will be marked to show which wire goes to which terminal so that the switch turns on the 'correct' way.

Two-way switching

The easiest way to run two-way switching is to use two-core and earth cable from the switch to the loop-in rose or junction box (as with one-way switching) and run a three-core and earth cable from the first two-way switch to the other.

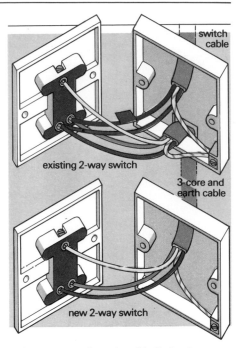

Three-core and earth cable links the two switches in a two-way switching circuit. The cores are colour coded for identification

Wiring a ceiling rose

Wiring a ceiling rose is straightforward providing you know which cable is which—it helps to label them as you go along. Pass all the cables through the backplate of the ceiling rose and then screw it to the ceiling before making the connection to the terminals. Make sure that the ladder you're standing on is secure and is standing level.

The cover of the ceiling rose should be slipped over the pendant flex before this is attached to the two outside terminals: it's easier to wire up the lampholder and strip the rose end of the flex before carrying it up to the ceiling. The two flex conductors are hooked over little lugs in the ceiling rose to carry the weight of the lamp and its lampshade. Make sure you have stripped enough sheathing to allow for this.

Fitting the switch

First you will have to make the hole in the wall to take the flush-mounted switch box—see Fitting boxes. The cable will need to be cut to the correct length to allow you sufficient room to make the connections but no so long that the switch faceplate can't be screwed to its box. This is particularly important if you're using plaster-depth boxes where there is less room behind the switch for the tangle of wires. The earth wire should be connected to the terminal on the box—it earths the fixing screws—and the red and black wires connected to the switch faceplate as described above.

Wall lights

The principle for wiring wall lights is exactly the same as for ceiling lights. The difference is that it will be easier to use a junction box in the loft or ceiling space and that you will need a special box for mounting the wall lights themselves—see pages 24 to 28 for more details.

Rewiring power circuits

In some ways, power circuits are easier to rewire than lighting circuits. But they need careful planning to get the sockets in the right place and to minimise the amount of cable used for the job.

Work out the number of socket outlets that you need—you can never have too many. You will also need to think carefully about where they're to be positioned. For most rooms, about 300mm above the floor is the usual position though old or disabled people will find it much easier if they're positioned higher up—say 1m above floor height. In the kitchen, the socket outlets should be about 150mm above the work surface (except for floor-standing appliances).

When planning the cable run, allow for any fused connection units for supplying fixed equipment. If you mark the positions of all these and all sockets on your room plans, you can work out how to run the circuit—in particular where the ring is to go and which sockets and connection units are to be fed from spurs connected to the ring.

Removing the old wiring

As with lighting circuits, the first thing to do is to make sure the existing circuit is completely dead by removing all the circuit fuses. Depending on how recently any additions were made to your power circuits, you may be able to use some or all of the existing PVC cable as part of your new circuit. But all rubber- or lead-sheathed cable should be removed, as should all round-pin sockets.

Leave cables which have been buried in walls—unless you're positioning the socket in the same place, in which case you must replace them. You'll have to lift floorboards

12 *Where cables run across the line of the joists, drill holes about 12mm in diameter and thread the cable through*

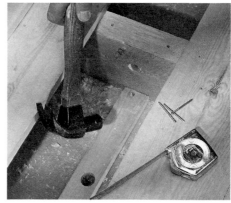

13 *At the position of each ceiling rose, nail a pre-drilled batten between the joists*

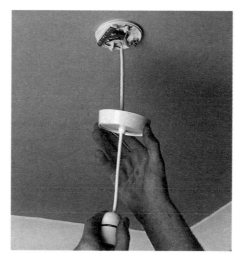

14 *Screw the rose in place and connect up the cables. Then add the flex. Check your electrical connections before you replace the rose cover*

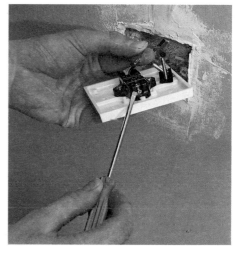

15 *At each switch position connect live and neutral switch cable cores to the terminals. Always make sure the cores are held securely*

to get at some of the cable which means clearing out at least some of the furniture and lifting up the carpet first.

Go round all the rooms marking the positions of the sockets on the walls with a pencil so that you can make the holes for flush mounting boxes. This can be hard and tedious work and it is probably best to work on one room at a time.

Running the cable

You must run 2.5mm² two-core and earth cable from the consumer unit position to the first and last sockets of the ring on the first floor. Later, when you come to do the downstairs ring the circuit cable will need to be run below the ground floor.

If, as is likely, the consumer unit is in the cupboard under the stairs, it should be possible to run the two cables directly into the space between the ground floor ceiling and the first floor floorboards.

Run the cable into the box for the socket and leave a short length hanging out for making the connections. Run another length of cable into the box, down under the floorboards and along to the position of the next socket. At sockets where you're fitting a spur, a third cable will need to be run from this position to that of the socket or fused connection unit on the spur.

Once all the cable is in place (see Routing cables) the next thing is to make good the plaster round the sockets and where cables have been chased into walls (with surface-mounted sockets, you don't have this problem). You can use metal or plastic conduit to protect the cables but it is acceptable simply to plaster over them—providing they run in straight and

16 *At each socket position, chop out the recess and the cable chase with a cold chisel and lump hammer. Then draw in the cables*

17 *Thread the cables into the box through one of the knockouts, strip the cores and connect them to the appropriate terminals*

18 *After making good, fold the cables neatly back into the mounting box and attach the faceplate. Check that it's level before it is finally tightened*

predictable lines downwards from the sockets (*never* horizontally) and that the cables are secured with clips before you cover them with plaster (you may need to chisel a bit of plaster away to fit the clips). Tuck the wires inside the boxes before replastering.

Wiring up a socket

The ends of each pair of red, black and earth (with yellow/green sleeving) wires should be twisted together using a pair of general-purpose pliers before putting them into the terminals and tightening the screw.

Once all the connections have been made, push the socket back into its box, making sure that the wires are not kinked or squashed, and secure the faceplate.

Routing cable and fitting boxes

Unless you run all the cables along the surface (which is unsightly), you're going to have to go through, across and along joists and through, up and down walls.

Joists: the easiest way to run cable is between the joists and under the floorboards. In the loft and under the first floor the cable should be clipped to the side of the joist at regular intervals. Underneath the ground floor (if it is a suspended timber floor) the cable can rest on the ground or be clipped to the sides of the joists or fixed to support battens nailed at right angles.

Running across joists is more difficult. In the loft, make use of the binders that run over the joists at right angles; below the first floor, you'll have to make holes in the joists. Make a hole with a brace and bit (or electric drill and wood bit) at least 50mm below the top of the joist to avoid damage from floorboard nails.

Walls: cutting channels (chases) in walls to run cables is one of the most time-consuming jobs in electric wiring. It has to be done accurately and carefully. The normal tool is a sharp bolster used with a club hammer. Mark the lines on the wall and cut down both lines before chiselling out between them with a cold chisel.

One problem area is getting the wires behind skirting boards. It's much easier if you take the skirting off, but this creates extra work in making good, particularly if you damage it getting it off. Alternatively, you can use a long masonry drill to make the hole in the wall *and* in the floorboard underneath.

You may have to remove the skirting if you have a solid ground floor so that you can run the cable round the walls behind the skirting.

In a stud partition wall, you may be able to run the cable up the space between the two sheets of plasterboard, but you may hit trouble in the form of noggins running horizontally between the vertical studs.

Mark the position of the box on the wall, making sure that the chase for the cable lines up with one of the entry holes in the box. Use a masonry bit and electric drill to make a honeycomb of holes the correct depth within the marked area to save on the chiselling necessary.

Once you've drilled all the holes, chisel away with your bolster to get a neat, square hole. Carry on chiselling until the box's front edge sits flush with or slightly before the surface.

Now drill and plug two holes in the wall behind the box to line up with the mounting holes in the box. The box should be secured with round-head screws though the plaster used to make good round the box will help hold it in place.

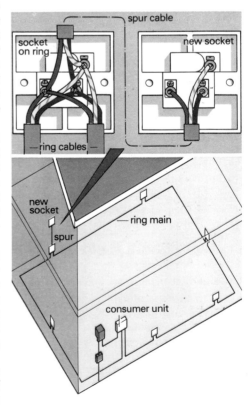

It's easiest to wire spurs from a socket on the ring main. The spur cable simply runs from the terminals of the ring main socket to the new outlet

Heavy duty circuits

Wiring a cooker is straightforward, but positioning the control unit needs careful thought.

You'll probably find that you don't need a very long length of $10mm^2$ (or $6mm^2$—see page 97) cable, which is just as well because it is quite expensive. The cooker control unit should be positioned so that it can be reached from where you stand in front of the cooker, preferably without having to reach over hot pans. If the control unit has a socket outlet, make sure that any flex runs from it would not be anywhere near the hot cooker rings.

The normal height for a cooker control unit is about 1.5m off the floor. The unit will need quite a large hole in the wall if it is to be flush mounted.

The supply cable is run from a 45 amp (or 30 amp) 'way' in the consumer unit to the control unit position. Another length of the same cable is run down from the cooker control unit to a cable outlet box mounted about 500mm above the floor; the cooker cable is then attached to this box. Unless this is vertically below the cooker control unit, this may involve chasing down to the floorboards and back up again to the outlet box to keep the runs vertical.

The connections inside the two boxes are simple: most control units have three terminals to which the cables coming from the consumer unit must be fitted; the cable running to the cooker or outlet box connects to three more terminals. The same applies to the outlet box, except that the three cores of the cables running from the control unit and the cooker will be connected to common terminals.

You may want to reorganise your cooker supply to power split-level units instead of a free-standing cooker. You can either link both components into a single cooker control unit, or run the circuit cable from the unit first to one component and then on to the other. In the first case, both components must be within 2m of the control unit; in the second case the component furthest from the control unit must be no more than 2m from it.

Immersion heaters and showers

Both of these systems demand their own electricity supplies—15 or 20 amps for the immersion heater, 30 amps for an electric shower—and these must be run direct from the consumer unit. Shower units must have a double-pole switch outside the bathroom or, in the form of a pull cord, inside. The immersion heater should be connected through a double-pole switch with flex outlet. Heat-resistant flex runs from this to the heater itself.

Fitting an ELCB

You may want to fit an earth leakage circuit breaker (ELCB)—also known as a residual current device (RCD)—as part of your re-wiring to protect certain parts of the system.

Some consumer units have ELCBs built in so that you can connect certain power circuits to them—the ones covering the kitchen and garage, say, plus any outside circuits. Alternatively, you can fit an ELCB immediately after the circuit fuseway and run the ring circuit on from there—use either a single $4.0mm^2$ cable or a pair of $2.5mm^2$ cables between the ELCB and the consumer unit and make sure that the circuit beyond is properly earthed—how you do this depends on the type of ELCB you're using. Most are fitted in a separate enclosure which needs to be bought separately.

If you want to protect only one or two sockets, you can use special socket outlets which include an ELCB built in. They're the size of a double socket, but have only one outlet. They're ideal for use in powering appliances being used out of doors.

The type of ELCB needed for these applications is a 30mA one with a loading appropriate for the socket or circuit.

Earthing and cross-bonding

It is absolutely essential that all the mains services—water and gas pipes—be earthed where they enter the house or as near to this point as possible. To do this, you run a $6mm^2$ single-core cable with green/yellow insulation to the pipes, where it is connected with a special bonding clamp; this has a label saying 'SAFETY ELECTRICAL CONNECTION DO NOT REMOVE'

In addition, all exposed metal which could conduct electricity should be earthed. The Electricity Board will advise what is necessary depending on your house and their earthing arrangements (and you must consult them as soon as you can), but as a minimum you should earth the water pipes leading to the hot and cold taps in the bathroom and kitchen, the central heating pipes and the hot water cylinder.

If cross-bonding has already been carried out as part of the previous installation, connect the cables to your main earthing point and have its efficiency checked by an expert. This is particularly important if any plastic plumbing has been used.

Fitting the consumer unit

Installing a consumer unit is a job that can be done in a day—you'll need to have the electricity disconnected.

When you are ready to install the new consumer unit, arrange for the Electricity Board to come in the morning to disconnect the electricity and again the evening to reconnect it. At this point you need to be sure that all your new work is electrically safe, and so you should test each completed circuit. There is a limit to the number of tests you can do yourself, but you should check polarity (all the wires connected to the correct terminals) and continuity (no breaks in the circuit). The first is mainly a matter of inspection; the second requires a simple continuity tester or multi-meter. Don't test for continuity with the power on. An electrician (or the electricity board) will carry out other tests to make sure that the circuit is safe for you.

The actual job of installing a new consumer unit was covered in detail on pages 84–88. Make sure you label each circuit as you connect it up to the unit.

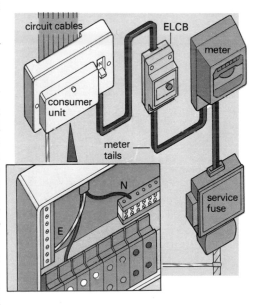

Within the consumer unit, the live cores go to individual fuseways, the others go to terminal blocks

INDEX